# Praise for *Relaxed Maximalism*

'Sarah's given us the most gorgeous guide to help us make our dream spaces in our homes a reality.'

—Georgia Willows, creator growth lead at Pinterest UK

'It's sensational to see Sarah's true style throughout her book. It's a beautiful read to inspire any home styling.'

—Sophia Hoddinott-Smith, brand marketing manager,
Anthropologie Europe

'A gorgeous must-read for anyone looking to infuse their home with personality and charm.'

—Dani Grande, associate producer, Homeworthy

'An inspirational guide for creating a house that feels like a home. Packed with personality and styling advice … it's a must read!'

—Maxine Brady and Gemma Gear, co-hosts, *How to Home Podcast*

'Escapism in a book! Sarah never fails to inspire and this beautiful guide will leave you feeling so much joy and optimism for your home.'

—That's so Gemma, Interior Stylist, @thatssogemma

# Relaxed Maximalism

# Relaxed Maximalism

## Curating a Maximalist Home with Soul

# Sarah Laming

**photography by Lou Souza**
**illustrations by Carlotta Spencer**

**mango**
PUBLISHING GROUP

MIAMI

For permission requests, please contact the publisher at:
Mango Publishing Group
5966 South Dixie Highway, Suite 300
Miami, FL 33143
info@mango.bz

For special orders, quantity sales, course adoptions and corporate sales, please email the publisher at sales@mango.bz. For trade and wholesale sales, please contact Ingram Publisher Services at customer.service@ingramcontent.com or +1.800.509.4887.

Relaxed Maximalism: Curating a Maximalist Home with Soul

Library of Congress Cataloging-in-Publication number: 2024940109
ISBN: (hc) 978-1-68481-644-6, (ebook) 978-1-68481-645-3
BISAC category code: ARC002000, ARCHITECTURE / Decoration & Ornament

Printed in the United States of America

*For Twiglet*

# Table of Contents

Chapter 1

# Opening thoughts

*A home is soul, vibe, and atmosphere.*

## A sense of home

You may live in a rambling house filled with period features, or a modern apartment in the heart of a city, or anywhere in-between. You may own it, or you may be renting it. It may be a chaotic house filled with young children, or a studio just for you. It doesn't matter where you live, or the type of house you live in; I believe anywhere has the potential to lift your spirits, to be a place where you can instantly relax and be a home that makes you smile.

You see, there's a big difference between a house and a home. A house is a structure made of bricks, but a home is where we live, embodying how we see ourselves—a space designed for life, not just for show. A house is merely a space to be painted, decorated, and filled with things. A home, however, is something else altogether. It's about soul, vibe, atmosphere, a feeling you can't quite put your finger on—a sense of *je ne sais quoi* that can only be captured with love and care.

A home is comfortable and comforting, bustling yet capable of being as relaxing as you wish. It's where you can kick off your shoes, curl up with a good book, or chat quietly with a soulmate. It's a place for welcoming friends and family around the kitchen table for suppers, where laughter fills the air late into the night, creating memories that last a lifetime.

Above all, a home is personal to you—a space you're proud of because it overflows with your personality. When friends visit, they know that it's you who lives there. It is unmistakably your space, it bears your stamp and tells your story, not that of an interior designer you hired, an influencer you follow, or the latest social media trend.

Suppers for friends.

# My Relax Max home

Mine is a busy family home, filled with pockets of calm. My colourful rooms are perfectly imperfect (to me) and would never claim to be finished! They evolve at their own pace and in their own time. I design my spaces so that the most beautiful spots are the spots we actually spend time in. Misplaced cushions sit alongside snuggly blankets beneath sunny windows. Rooms are filled with a curious blend of antiques from Asia and bright, British classics picked up in department stores. A giant Paddington Bear from the 1950s sits alongside a wicker elephant table. It's rather a mismatch, but it's a harmonious one, and it's totally me!

About fifteen years ago, when I began decorating our family house, there was no Pinterest or Instagram or TikTok. Neutral, Scandi-style, minimalist homes dominated most of the glossy mags. Most sofas were grey, most bathrooms were beige, and ceilings were filled with recessed downlighting. These homes were beautiful, they were impeccably styled, they were "perfect."

But they didn't intrigue me or fill my heart with joy, and I knew I didn't want to live in one. They didn't feel like places where I would ever be able to relax. They were too designed, too perfect, too formal. Not me!

So, I went back to the past and found inspiration in old English country houses; homes that had been in families for generations, where furniture told stories through scratches and bumps, where rooms were colourful, and floral designs were on paintings, walls, and sofas. It was a time before recessed lighting was ever a thing. Lamps sat in pools of welcoming light and shelves of books lay waiting to be explored. They were homes that were rich in history, colour, and pattern, and they were relaxing places. There, no one was going to worry about a cushion that had been squashed, an abandoned pair of shoes, or a half-finished book on the arm of the sofa.

Wicker elephant sits next to a floral chair.

These homes became my starting point, but how could I translate them into my home for now, for life in the twenty-first century?

Florals and dogs bring a sense of nostalgia!

I began by painting a single room and buying a floral sofa (because I just love floral sofas)! Then I bought some teapot-shaped lights to hang above my kitchen table. Sure enough, I began to fall in love. My confidence grew, my style developed, and I went on some courses to learn about design rules and hear about the rich history of interior design.

Inspired by that history, I began to work out how to create my home for today. A home that draws from the past and yet never seems dated. A place that is nostalgic but sits comfortably with the present day, with modern life. A home where a shiny new lamp sits happily on a vintage table.

I have been lucky enough to travel quite a lot in my life and spent several years living in Southeast Asia. Many of my purchases from that part of the world—mostly heritage pieces—have become a big part of my house today. A place where a Chinese medicine chest sits proudly in my hall alongside a North African rug and an English dresser!

I've ended up creating a home that is a beautiful, eclectic but lived-in space; an honest reflection of my life and loves. *I*s remain undotted and *T*s remain uncrossed, but I love it anyway. I don't yearn for that perfection. I'm happy with the perfectly imperfect.

This journey I have been on is mostly captured on Instagram, where I have been posting pictures of my house since 2019. This was always intended to be just a personal passion project—honestly! But as time went by, I could see that other people were interested in this style too. As I write this, I have over 1.1 million followers and a deep sense of imposter syndrome!

As you can imagine, I've learned so much over the past years and I'm delighted to have this opportunity to pass this knowledge on. So, let's start by explaining my style, Relaxed Maximalism.

The angle of the chair makes all the difference.

# What is Relaxed Maximalism?

Maximalism, as an interiors style, has been around for centuries. Some of our first famous Maximalists were the Victorians who filled their homes with rich, colourful fabrics and their cabinets with curiosities from around the world. Since then, Maximalism has fallen in and out of fashion and taken different forms. Ranging from the faded glories of English country houses in post war Britain, to the clashing colours and bold patterns of the Memphis Group who stormed through the 1980s with their rebellious, rule-breaking design ethos.

Having lost out to the pared-back, everything-in-a-drawer minimalism of the 2000s, maximalist interiors are now making a full-on comeback, currently taking Instagram and TikTok by storm. So, just quickly, what is a maximalist interior? And how does Relaxed Maximalism differ?

Maximalism, inevitably, doesn't have a neat and tidy definition! There are many routes you can follow when creating a maximalist interior—but central to each of them is the art of layering colour, pattern, and texture. There is always a focus on creating interiors which are joyful and full of personality. All maximalist designers talk of mixing styles and eras, combining old and new, adding a bit of whimsy or something irreverent. And all maximalist interiors have a spirit of "more is more."

But, right now, a lot of these maximalist interiors are loud, attention-seeking rooms that don't hold back. Bright colours run riot across floors and walls and ceilings. Patterns clash, rooms are bold and flamboyant. These interiors have enormous personalities.

Two Staffordshire dogs
and a mantelpiece.

Home is a person, a cake, and a dog.

Much as I can totally appreciate this kind of maximalism, and whilst I love looking at these exuberant and creative interiors, I couldn't actually live in one! It does not mean "home" to me.

I think there is a way of doing maximalism that creates a quieter, more relaxing home. I call it Relaxed Maximalism (or Relax Max for short).

Relaxed Maximalism is a philosophy that believes you should always create a home to make you smile, that reflects your personality, your personal history, and that makes you happy. It follows the principles of adding more to our homes, but with clear guidelines for how to keep a beautiful style.

It loves adding colour but uses it with restraint. It adds multiple patterns, but in ways that they harmonise, not clash. It draws what we love from the world, welcoming the eclectic and individual, but always with some coherence to tether the style.

Relaxed Maximalism invites "more" into a home, but always "more of yourself." It creates a home filled with your own personal soul, brimming with your rich stories and self-expression. It nods to trends but is more inspired by your own history and personal style. Our homes are designed not to be on-trend, but on-us.

Relax Max homes are harmonious and joyful, they take effort, but look effortless; chairs are comfortable, rugs are faded, books and flowers combine to create a sense of romance and nostalgia.

Whilst my Relax Max style applies to my home, I often get glimpses of its relevance more widely. Any point of view about *home* is always going to be somewhat related to our lives more generally and how we lead them. Many of its urges and principles can be applied to other things too; how we dress, how we cook, the places we go, the lifestyle choices we make. I might even call myself a Relaxed Maximalist!

So, I'd like to represent Relaxed Maximalism in a manifesto form to reflect how much I believe in it as a beautiful way of think and make choices in life!

# The Relax Max Manifesto

A house must be a home.

Designed for life, not show.

It should be filled with your personality and soul.

Brimming with rich stories and self-expression.

Never slavishly on-trend, but always 'on you.'

You draw what you love from the world;
eclectic and individual, perfectly imperfect,

just loosely tethered by your sense of story-full
whimsy and soul.

You surround yourself with layers of the
things that have meaning.

Curated slowly and layered gradually.

You fuse, you blend, you mix.
It's eclectic, but personal.

It's a place where you always feel comfortable,

It's a home to make you smile.

# Welcome to the journey

If you have picked up this book, I'm guessing that you don't want a minimalist, perfect-looking home, where everything has its place or is hidden in a drawer! Polished, neat, immaculate styling just isn't your cup of tea. Perhaps the Relax Max look might work better for you.

How do you create your own Relax Max home—a space that is uniquely yours but doesn't feel cluttered or overwhelming? If you are steering clear of minimalism, how do you not have a messy home? How do you strike the balance between carefree, casual décor and a sense of order? How do you mix pattern, colour and texture without it feeling chaotic? Where on earth do you even begin?!

Relax Max embraces the fact that transforming the look and feel of your home is not a task, it's a glorious journey—one that's deeply personal. This journey holds the potential to infuse your home with something special, making it as unique as you are.

In this book, my aim is to offer guidance and inspiration on this journey— for you to make your home truly yours, a place you love. Remember, it won't always be perfect! Your home may (hopefully) have its imperfections, bumps, and scratches, and no doubt some unfinished jobs, but it will always be stylish and inspiring. Above all, it will be uniquely you!

But don't worry, I won't leave you hanging when it comes to the specifics. I'll delve into the particular choices you'll need to make in certain areas: how to choose colours and mix patterns, how to layer décor and style corners, and how to craft rooms that feel cosy yet whimsical. I'll guide you on finding vintage treasures and combining them with modern, practical buys. With these insights, I hope you'll be well-equipped to create your own "Relax Max" home—a home that makes you smile.

*Sarah x*

---

Some shoes for the journey.

# Chapter 2

# Plan for your head and your heart

*Home is about the people who live there, and their individual lives, hope and dreams.*

I'm all for spontaneity, but I wouldn't advocate that you dive headlong into decoration without quite a bit of thought first. I understand how eager one can feel about transforming a house into a dream home, but don't just start! Don't just jump into buying things and painting rooms!

This is not only advice for people who are tackling a whole-house renovation. It is equally relevant for smaller projects like adding character to a single room. Whatever your circumstances, it's important to take a little bit of time to do some planning first and to set yourself up for what's ahead.

Planning for a Relax Max home is about two things; planning a home that *works* for you, but it's also planning a home that is *about* you.

Stylish work!

There is a functional side to how a home needs to work. Its spaces will have some existing features and some practical constraints. These are like the "bones" of your house that you must work with and design harmoniously around, making every room work in the best possible way for your lifestyle. And, of course, everyone's real-life requirements will differ wildly, from a big family to a young student, and so it needs to work for everyone.

But, often overlooked, is an *emotional* side of planning a home; how your home *feels* and how it is uniquely *your* home and reflective of *your* story. It is *about* you. A home that is reminiscent of you is a place where you can be the most comfortable and happiest version of yourself. This is something to weave throughout the practical aspects of every room and corner.

Planning the basics of your home should take both these perspectives into account. If you just plan around the functionality of your home, then you will have something very practical, but rather impersonal. Equally, if you only plan for the emotional side of your home, it will feel unique but won't be easy to live in!

We will look at this balance, or Yin Yang, of the practical and personal throughout this chapter. It will involve careful, practical thought plus a bit of self-reflection. It shouldn't feel prescriptive though, and it really is very flexible once you know the basics—consider it a voyage of discovery!

Get this planning right and it will help you with all the hundreds of decisions that will come later. It will mean that whenever you are faced with choosing a chair, or fabric, or paint colour, you will be able to ask yourself, "Is this me?" "Does it suit my style?" and "Will this work?" Early planning will make each decision a little bit easier and ultimately help to avoid making those decisions that you end up regretting.

Flower power.

## Feelings matter

Interiors books tend to talk a lot about, well, Interiors! They focus on the stuff inside a house—the architecture, paint colours, furniture, fixtures, fittings, art accessories, layout. (And don't worry, in this book, I will also be talking about all these things too!)

But there is a danger that this ignores the fact that the inside of a house is not just about the stuff put inside it, but about the people who live there, and their individual lives, hope and dreams.

So, at the heart of this book, will be the philosophy that no matter how beautiful the room, it will feel empty if it isn't filled with the souls of the people who live, love and make memories in it. Our feelings and emotions should be as rooted in our homes as our paint colours.

Because home isn't just a place, it's also a feeling. A feeling which is so personal, intangible, and evocative that it means very different things to different people.

Understanding how *you* want *your* home to feel means that you will have the foundations to make your home somewhere that makes you feel happy, and that enables you to be your most comfortable version of yourself. Ultimately, it means that, even if the place you are living in isn't your dream house it will always feel like *you*...and it will feel like the best version of your home from the moment you walk through the front door.

I asked my Instagram followers what "home" means to them; they chose these words and this word cloud.

Reading, not decorating.

# What does home mean to you?

So, before you dive into buying paint and furniture, give some thought to what home means to you, capture the essence of that in a few words or phrases, and remind yourself with every decision you make!

I also asked my Instagram followers to describe what home meant to them. Here are just a few of the many I received. How beautifully they capture the essence of home.

# Home is...

- Where your soul can have a nap

- The chime of Grandma's cuckoo clock at noon

- A place I am always happy to return to

- Where Mum is

- A hug from a loved one after a long day

- A place you can just be

- Sliding my feet into cosy slippers

- Waggling tails after a long day at work

- Where everything feels just right

- People gathered around the table

- Coffee in bed

- Coming into the house and falling perfectly onto the furniture

- A sofa, my books and a nap

- Kids playing cricket in the kitchen

- The smell of raw mango with spices

- Sinking into your bed after the longest day

- Where I can wear my pyjamas all day long

- Like taking off a heavy winter coat because it's warm enough there without it

- My husband singing in the morning

- A cosy, slightly messy place

- Cooking the Sunday Roast whilst watching Super Sunday

- Where I can be unapologetically me

- The first bite of sticky toffee pudding

- Sisters chatting

- Where I can exist without being judged

- The sound of laughter from the kitchen

- A cosy blanket on a rainy day

- Hearing the key in the door followed by "hello Mum"

- The kettle boiling

- Where the world quiets down for a moment

- Cinnamon rolls baking on a Sunday morning

# The character of your home

Now that you have ideas for how you want your home to feel, it's time to consider the property itself—when it was built, its location, its style, and its character. A Relax Max home must work in harmony with, and not fight against, the physical place in which you're living.

This does not mean that you should create a homage to a particular period. Ugh! I just think that the décor of a house works best when it is sympathetic to the house itself. Nailing this bit of thinking helps (once again) with all those decisions you will have to make further down the line—colour choices, wallpaper, furniture styles.

Take colour, for example. You may decide you want to paint a room pink. But there are hundreds of pinks to choose from. So, knowing the style and age of your property can help you to narrow down those choices. A heritage pink might look fabulous in the bedroom of a period property, but a more modern pastel pink may suit a more modern townhouse.

Windowed wonderland!

# A focus on features

Tea lights and weathered wood.

It's also important to consider the features of the room you are planning to decorate. Rooms in period properties will usually have some relatively traditional features—a fireplace, bay windows, original floorboards, or corniced ceilings. A modern apartment, on the other hand, may not have any of these "traditional" features, but it will have something else: a big expanse of wall, perhaps, the perfect spot for a piece of art or two, a window with a view, or maybe, even, a little balcony.

If you have the luxury of time, consider the intangible features too; things that change across seasons. We lived in our house for a whole year before we made any changes. So, by the time the builders arrived, we knew it intimately—the sunny spots, and cosy corners, the way the light fell in different rooms at different times of the day or year. But what we had really fallen in love with was the view from our windows, and how it changed from winter though to summer and back again.

As you may know from my Instagram, the windows in my house have become an integral feature within the design of our rooms. We chat in front of them, read beside them, dogs look out of them, and storms batter into them. We watch the seasons through them and decorate for the seasons around them. There is always someone in front of one of our windows.

So, look for the special features of your unique rooms and make them your stars. Then plan for them too, making sure they aren't forgotten or hidden, but are part of your designs.

Windows can be features.

# Design for living

Considering how you are going to use your room is the moment when you need to be as practical and honest about your lifestyle as you can. Plan for the life you are living now and be realistic. If you have small children, maybe don't plan a formal sitting room! Think about how you would spend your perfect weekend afternoon, or your ideal evening in the kitchen. What is your best bedtime routine? Be honest here too. Plan for the weekday evenings you actually have—do you eat at the table or are you frequently sat on the sofa in front of the latest box set? Would you love a corner dedicated to you, a book nook for reading, or a desk for when you WFH? The more honest you are, the more you can arrange your home to work for you, at each point in your day.

Folding dining tables create extra space and an extra shelf!

# Get inspired and find your style

## Pinterest

In the days before social media, I mostly scoured magazines for ideas on how to decorate my house, filling scrapbooks with the pictures I'd torn from my favourite magazines—*Living etc.*, *World of Interiors*, *Homes and Gardens*. But once these pictures were glued down, the pages were decided. Even though they looked gorgeous, it was impossible to rearrange, delete, or move a picture from one place to another. It was hard to zoom in on a corner or save my favourite lamp in a gazillion places. It was hard to get an overview of the whole thing—or change my mind!

But now you can pick up your mobile and, within a moment, search for ideas via a hashtag or colour, object, or style. Type in a keyword and you are bombarded with a hundred ideas on Google, Pinterest, Instagram, and TikTok. (You can even write prompts into the generative AI applications.) Not only can you follow the people whose style you love—you can message them, ask questions, build a relationship. Best of all, you can file posts on Instagram and build boards on Pinterest.

Pinterest is now my favourite way of mood boarding, and putting together Pinterest boards is a great way of finding your own sense of style. It's my go-to place to gather inspiration for rooms, corners, shelves, sofas, rugs, colours. It's the place where I can really begin to envisage how I want a space to look and feel.

So, gather the pictures that you like for each of your rooms, and as you continue, you will find that you are drawn to the same thing over and over again, building up a vision of your ideal space or corner.

---

Mood boarding on a table.

Make sure you send everything to your Pinterest board, so that it is all in one place. You can add pins to a board from Pinterest itself, from websites and if you find something you love in a magazine, or whilst you are out and about, take a photo of it and send that to Pinterest too.

Then narrow it down a bit and create some very specific boards. Get into the details—lights, rugs, tiles, whatever you like.

The joy of these Pinterest boards is that they are so flexible—you can delete the things you no longer like and add in something that you do. They are always on your mobile, so always with you. You can also share your boards with anyone and reference them at any moment.

## Gather your confidence

I'd like to tell you how my own confidence in design and creativity has developed over the years, as I think it suggests there is hope for anyone!

Growing up, I was genuinely awful at drawing and painting. My focus was on reading rather than art. I spent my spare time curled up on a sofa with my nose in an Enid Blyton book, not sitting at the table with paintbrushes, sticks of glue, and scissors. Art was the subject I dreaded the most at school, and I gave it up as soon as I could. As I wasn't good at art, I left education thinking that I wasn't a creative person. If you had told the fifteen-year-old me that the incredibly creative worlds of interiors and social media would become my job, I would probably have laughed in disbelief.

It wasn't until we bought our first flat and had the opportunity to decorate it that I realised I had clear ideas about how I wanted my home to look. It started with a feeling that I did not want my flat to look the same as everyone else's flat! Only then did I realise that being creative wasn't all about being able to draw or paint, it was about having ideas and an imagination. And so began my journey into interior decorating.

Create a little vignette.

My style has developed since those early days, and I have made plenty of mistakes along the way. That first flat ended up with a red bathroom, which would have been okay if it were a nice red, or it didn't clash horribly with the avocado bathroom suite we couldn't afford to replace. About ten years ago, I painted virtually half my house a dreary shade of grey when grey was a thing. Those rooms were truly miserable. And in my pursuit of the unique, I have ended up buying uncomfortable chairs with no springs, just because I like the fabric, or old metal tables which are unusable because of rust!

But here's the thing—these mistakes have been invaluable lessons. Although I've completed courses on interior decoration, I still make choices based more on intuition (the touchy-feely kind) than on strict measurements—just like everyone does! Some mistakes I've learned to live with (even the red bathroom stayed for a while), and others I've quickly changed. Throughout this journey, I've experimented, tried new things, bought what I love, and ultimately created rooms I adore, no matter where they may be.

I tell you this story to make the point that if the "fifteen-year-old, un-creative me" can turn into a person who can decorate a stylish home, then so can you. Indeed, I believe anyone, with a little effort and inspiration, can create rooms they love. I'm not saying that it is easy, the process is a little tricky at times. However, it does become easier with practice and then, quite suddenly, you are decorating your rooms with confidence—enjoying the moments of joy that come with creating a space that truly feels yours.

So, let's delve into the nitty gritty of how to decorate a home, remembering that you don't need to be a professional to create rooms you love. What you do need is a dash of confidence and a grasp of the basics.

Let's begin.

Reflections.

# Chapter 3

# Recurring themes

*Home is full of micro stories, small behaviours, and fleeting moments.*

It is important to remember that our homes aren't merely a cluster of disconnected spaces. We move constantly between our rooms and so a home should have a sense of cohesion about it. There needs to be a connection between the bathroom and the kitchen, the bedroom and the sitting room, so that each room feels like it is part of the same "family." This unity brings a comforting familiarity across the home, linking the emotions and atmosphere throughout.

I think of these qualities that exist across a home as *themes*. These are the aspects of styling that cut across individual rooms, furniture, and features. They can apply to almost anything you are tackling and can work in any room.

As you will see, themes are not physical items or precise art direction. They are emotional qualities that offer a consistency of personality or vibe in a Relax Max home.

Vintage finds.

# A personal note

I'm very fortunate and grateful to have a significant following on social media—you may have even bought this book because you follow me @ ahometomakeyousmile. The comments and messages that I receive most often are about how my videos make people *feel*. I am frequently told that they bring a moment of peace and tranquillity amidst the hustle and bustle of daily life. My home often resonates with recollections of childhood, evoking memories of mothers, or long-ago summers spent with grandmas. By the way, this feedback is what makes managing my social media accounts such a rewarding and delightful experience.

Other comments convey the notion that people can *connect* with me just through seeing my rooms and feeling their atmosphere. That is because my house is deeply personal. It is filled with those intimate touches that evoke that unmistakable sense of "home." My well-thumbed books rest open on sofas, or form inviting piles on coffee tables. My art, collected over decades, is propped casually on windowsills and floors; there's always a decorative rug from a far-flung market I have visited. And, there's frequently a colourful mug of my morning tea just waiting to be finished. All these elements impart a lingering essence of the person (me!) who has recently occupied the room or is on the brink of returning to that spot on the unusual floral sofa, or the slightly rumpled bed.

Even though there is no one actually visible in the videos, it is this almost tangible sense of the person who lives there that give the videos such significant emotional value.

There's a strong sense of the person who lives here,
even though you can't see them.

Now, I'm not suggesting that you intentionally embrace an entirely dishevelled, lived-in home with unmade beds and unfinished cups of tea—let's reserve that for the videos! But it is these small, authentic touches, alongside a home that is forgiving of a little bit of mess (and isn't too perfect), that, I believe, truly transforms a house into a warm and welcoming home.

You see, all too often, our books just stand neatly in a straight line on bookshelves, treasures picked up on those holidays of yesteryear languish forgotten in a drawer, a childhood collection gathers dust in an attic, and all our photographs reside unseen inside our phones.

But these are the things that tell your unique story—the tales of who you are, the places you've ventured and the passions that stir your heart. Your home is the one place you can put them all, because your home is about you. It's the place where you get to decide what matters most!

So, fill it with these things, these things that are you. Fill it so that when a friend comes through your door, they don't see a trend, or a designer, they see *you*, unapologetically, in every corner and every detail of your home.

# A sense of history

I have a green velvet chair which sits beside our fireplace. It bears a slightly sagging seat and there is the conspicuous absence of a button, or two. Before it came to us, this chair sat in every house my parents lived in. Following in my father's footsteps, my son now dedicates Sunday afternoons to watching football from it. On wintry evenings, it's the spot where I lose myself in books, or the latest episode of a reality TV series—just as my mother did before me. Generations of dogs have curled up on its fading cushions too.

Jack's old chair.

Next to this little chair is a rug. It's one of the many rugs I bought on holidays to Morocco. This particular one came from a carpet shop in Fez's ancient medina. The elderly shopkeeper had bought it from a market in the Atlas Mountains where it had been meticulously woven by women from the Beni Ourain tribes. My rug is quite old, not *really* old, but about forty years old. I often think about where it has been before. I ponder the woman who wove it, and the elements of her life she may have infused into the design.

In another room, I have my 1950s Paddington collection box. I found him at Ardingly Antiques Fair one freezing February morning. I fell in love with him immediately but almost let him go due to a blunt comment from my friend who found him "old and dusty"—rude! For just a moment, I turned away, but I soon went back. Thank goodness. He makes me smile every single time I catch sight of him, and because he always makes me smile, he inspired the name of my Instagram account @ahometomakeyousmile. I believe that you need to fill your home with things that make you smile!

**Constant friends.**

You see, this embracing of the past lends a sense of comfort and reassurance to a Relax Max home. History, heritage, roots, and character hold a profound sway over us all. Whether rooted in personal memories, historical origins, or the tales that these items could tell (those missing buttons or events woven into their soul), they remind us of a world beyond ourselves and of our place in time.

In our fast-paced present, these nostalgic glimpses of a "golden age," when life seemed to be simpler and more organic, offer a sense of solace, irrespective of the actual historical reality.

# Joy in the little things

When the world around me becomes a bit too much, I instinctively reach for a book. I always have. Getting lost in its pages allows me to momentarily forget everything and immerse myself in pure joy. It always used to be an actual physical book; now it's usually my Kindle. I don't know if this is a good thing or a bad thing, it's just a thing.

Other things that bring me joy are spring bulbs—you know, the ones I grow in a mish-mash of pots all around my house. The first colourful bud, peeking through in the depths of winter, brings with it a burst of delight, as does every flower that follows. The wind playing tricks with my curtains brings me joy, and so do windy winter storms outside my window. The sort of storms that happen when I am tucked safely inside with a flickering candle (not outside having forgotten my umbrella)! Candles always make me smile. I appreciate their flicker at dusk but love how they fill a room with their lingering scent. There's one particular candle that I buy for every Christmas. It lasts months beyond the holiday season, and so, even in June, I light it and get a sudden burst of Christmassy pleasure.

Candles at dusk.

In our house we have little fights over little things like these. Those tug-of-wars you have in a marriage. Take hand wash. My husband buys antibacterial, antiseptic, anti-everything hand wash. There is no germ in this world that would survive a blob of his hand wash and a splash of scalding water. On the other hand, I like hand wash with the scent of mandarin rind, or rosemary leaf, or geraniums in summer—hand washes that are gentle on the environment, kind to animals, and soft on my skin. We compromise, of course; his hand wash is in the kitchen, mine is in the downstairs cloakroom. What he doesn't know is that I never use his hand wash, because my hand wash always brings me a moment's joy and his absolutely doesn't!

Floral handwash,
floral loo.

It's these little things, that bring these joyful moments, that I like to have to hand at home. Reminding myself that a house can be series of delightful little steps that take joy in the small things. It's not just the big experience of entering a house and having a "wow" room. Life at home is full of micro stories, small behaviours, and fleeting moments. Cherish them all, and design your house to make those small things work and feel special.

Pleasure in the mundane as well as the exciting is what makes life richer, especially as none of these things are necessarily expensive. It just takes a moment to work out what they are and to put them in place. So, it doesn't matter how you are feeling, be it happy or sad, it's still possible to feel moments of pure joy in a Relax Max house. You just need to get into the habit of appreciating those small moments of pleasure that bubble up without warning or planning, but which can contribute more to lasting happiness than those grand days that only come around so rarely.

# Slow decorating and sustainability

By nature, I am moderately lazy. I enjoy lie-ins on Sunday mornings and rereading books by Elizabeth Jane Howard. I like watching the gradual shift in seasons through my windows and the sunlight dancing on my sofa. I love taking Twiglet for a walk, and I would far rather have a long lunch with friends than paint a bedroom. Even though I don't like shopping very much—I agonise over even the smallest decision—wandering around flea markets is one of my favourite pastimes. I worry about waste and throwing things away and I don't like rushing, it makes me anxious.

As you have probably guessed, all of these things mean that I am not one for following the latest decorating trends. Before you know it, the latest trend turns into the next latest trend, necessitating yet another round of painting. Sigh. Or a new sofa, chosen in the latest colour, becomes last year's colour and is suddenly "out of date"—a far more expensive "out of date" than that jar of spices languishing at the back of the cupboard.

So, for me personally, it's much more satisfying to embrace a far more planet-friendly, laid-back attitude to decorating, making the most of more thoughtful and unhurried choices. I like to think of it as long, languorous, lazy decorating—investing effort once and keeping it for as many years as is feasible. No decorating happens in my house on a whim, which, quite possibly, I take to extremes. I decorate only when a room becomes almost unbearable to live in—primarily because I loved how it was decorated in the first place.

Likewise, I try to buy wisely and less frequently, making sure that I always love what I buy. So, once I have the basics in place, I don't worry if I haven't happened upon the perfect chair for that unloved corner, or a painting for a particular spot, because the joy is in the journey. I'm also not particularly drawn to brand new items I could nip down to a high street to buy on a Saturday afternoon. I love those vintage pieces that, at times, tend to find me when the time is right, rather than me trying to find them. Maybe it will be later this month, or possibly next year, but not to worry, I know I will love it more once it eventually reveals itself.

The table and chair that found me via my friend Anna.

# A big hug

Once, I attempted to count the number of throws and blankets strewn across my sofas and beds. I lost count when I ran out of fingers. You would be forgiven for thinking that I have so many because I am always cold, although that is indeed true! In fact, my husband even joked in his wedding speech, on a chilly January day in England, that he thought I might walk down the aisle swathed in a "bridal duvet" instead of a wedding dress. (At least I hope it was a joke!)

But, whilst staying warm is undoubtedly a significant reason for my fondness for sofa blankets, it's not the sole one. Throws, to me, represent more than just warmth and comfort; they embody cosiness and create a welcoming atmosphere in a room. They are vital ingredients to a space that feels as though it's ready to envelop you in a giant, comforting hug. When you walk into a room and spot a sofa full of throws and blankets, it's as if the room is saying, "I want you to relax, to feel warm and at ease. This is a place where kicking off your shoes and curling up on a sofa is not just allowed, it's encouraged."

When the world outside feels chaotic, or disheartening, or even just after a busy day at work, we instinctively seek solace in our homes, and these blankets and throws are just one symbol of the comfort we can create—that atmosphere of a home that gives us a warm and fuzzy feeling. The rest is about achieving casual imperfection with cushions, blankets, books, and harmonious layers of patterns that blend seamlessly. It's about designing rooms that don't disrupt, overwhelm or clash but instead offer comfort, tranquillity and reassurance.

To experience cosiness, we needn't be nestled beside a roaring log fire, although that is undeniably delightful when possible. It's also possible to create a similar sensation by making sure our rooms are lit with pools of welcoming light, are decorated in colours that we love, and are filled with texture and little imperfections.

---

Blankets make cosy.

# A touch of whimsy

Aged twenty, I moved to London and found myself sharing a flat in Notting Hill with a girl called Sancie. It was without doubt one of the most remarkable places I've ever called home.

Our flat was officially one bedroom, but had been cleverly converted for two enormous beds. The first bed was perched on a mezzanine above the sitting room, accessible by a rather rickety ladder—not designed for post-evening-out climbs! The second bed, surprisingly, was a huge window seat in the actual bedroom, with a lumpy mattress for sleep and enormous old shutters for curtains. Beyond an ancient kitchen was a slender strip of a balcony, just wide enough to enjoy a cup of tea—whilst offering a view of the ever-present ever-armed policeman. You see, Princes William and Harry attended a school on the same street, so there was always a guard. Our flat was owned by a lady called Sophie, who had recently returned from her time living with the Orange People cult in India. It was an eclectic and marvellously eccentric flat, and living there was an absolute delight.

The next best thing about this flat was its location right at the top of Portobello Road, right by the famous market. This was long before the *Notting Hill* movie and before the politicians and pop stars moved in. Instead, it was a time when boutique shops, gastro pubs, and trendy restaurants were just starting to appear. Our Saturday mornings often revolved around exploring the market, looking for bargains and antiques, and drinking wine at restaurants called "Wine Gallery."

It was on one of these Saturday mornings that I stumbled across a cabbage-shaped salad bowl that I still have today. It's a beautiful bowl, even if it doesn't sound it! I later learned that it comes from the Bordallo Pinheiro pottery in northern Portugal, a pottery I now love for its unique and yet incredibly stylish creations. They still make these bowls, along with platters shaped like pumpkins and jugs decorated with little strawberries. My cabbage bowl embodies character and a touch of quirk, and it's totally me. It's the kind of bowl that is fabulous for dinner parties because it makes even a bag of salad leaves look nice and your table look jolly.

Cabbage-leaf bowl.

I think that living in that flat helped me to appreciate the delightfully unconventional. And, whilst I can't create mezzanines and window seat beds, I've managed to infuse a touch of quirkiness, like that small salad bowl, into every room in my home. Over my dining room table, I've hung teapot-shaped lights. There's an elephant table made from wicker in front of my bookcase; he serves as the perfect spot for a lamp and a book. Our big hallway light requires an enormous lampshade, and I found one of those made from ostrich feathers! Additionally, there are the floral sofas beneath each of my downstairs windows. You can spot decorative dogs and brass elephants on tables and windowsills; they sit alongside a trio of concrete mushrooms. At one point we even had a flying trapeze, thanks to my adventurous daughter!

These are my troves of treasure, the unique pieces that breathe a sense of playfulness into my rooms. The things that infuse my home with a carefree and light-hearted atmosphere because they don't take themselves too seriously. In the same way that I prefer casual and slightly unconventional outfits over a carefully tailored look in my clothes, it is this same casualness and individual style that I seek in my living spaces.

To me, a meticulously decorated room, where everything matches perfectly, where there is no element of surprise or nothing unexpected, can feel a little dull—somewhat soulless, or like it is trying too hard. Incorporating a quirky element, an odd one out, on the other hand, reveals the playful side of your home and your personality. These pieces embody the casual, joyful essence of life—introducing a touch of imperfection, giving you the opportunity to take a second look and smile!

Teapot lights.

The key to striking the right balance, though, is to make thoughtful choices; choose wisely and choose only the things that truly resonate with you, rather than incorporating quirkiness for its own sake. And keep these pieces to a select few. You're not aiming for a wild and wacky home that's merely peculiar; instead, you're aiming for a home that is full of character and consistently delivers delightful surprises.

# Outside-inside

I cannot write about the elements of a Relax Max interior without delving into the significance of the *outside* and its presence *inside* my house.

As I scroll through my Instagram grid, brimming with images and videos of my home, I am consistently struck by the love for my windows and the outdoor scenes they frame. These views hold a special place in the hearts of observers, for they show the passage of British seasons and the ever-changing spectacle of English weather!

But it's not just my followers who appreciate my windows—these are the sunny spots our whole family naturally gravitate to; we watch the passing of time through the changing leaves on the trees outside. I have become attuned to these annual rhythms: in October, the leaves turn slowly from green to gold; by November, they boast a full spectrum of autumnal reds and browns. In December, the branches stand bare. The magnolia tree blossoms in March and, come April, the gig tree boasts its first leaves. Come July, the trees create a lush canopy in the sky.

Inside, on windowsills and tables, the first hyacinths make their appearance in time for Christmas, followed swiftly by daffodils, then anemones in February or March. As spring turns to summer and the choices become abundant—pelargoniums run riot. By November, my ever-loyal pink geranium is the sole remaining flower, basking in its sunny spot year-round.

Sunny spots.

What I am getting at here is that, regardless of your window's size or the view it offers, you can find your own ways to invite the outdoors in and still savour the seasonal rhythms. These natural changes serve as beautiful timekeepers and nourishment for the soul. You don't necessarily need a scenic view of leaves changing on trees, because cultivating potted flowers can be equally rewarding. (Here's a secret: I don't grow mine from seed; I buy them as sprouting bulbs from flower shops and garden centres—I'm not that green-fingered!) And if you don't want pots, just small bunches of seasonal flowers in vintage vases, or even jam jars, adds a similar feel.

Yet, it's not only the window view or the changing seasons that capture our imagination; it's always the harmonious blend of the interior and its deep connection to the exterior that resonates.

Let's consider those videos for a moment—outside, we witness the seasons, weather, trees, and sunshine. Inside, there are pages of a book that flutter in a breeze, the gentle glow of a candle on the windowsill juxtaposed with the storm that rages just on the other side. These same windowsills brim with those pots of seasonal flowers. It's the undeniable pull to this "outside-inside" aesthetic that has led me to really appreciate the joys of this interaction between the indoors and outdoors.

So, make the most of your light-filled and sunny spaces; put a sofa or chair in front of a window and treat it like a sunroom. Think carefully about how you frame your windows. Infuse your space with nature using floral fabrics or bold leaf prints—they needn't cover entire sofas; a cushion will do the trick. Explore floral wallpapers, or a bunch of faux flowers, to brighten up even the darkest corners, and make space for plants, large or small, whether they be spider or fiddle-leaf figs. The weekly ritual of watering becomes a rhythm of its own, giving the indoors a genuine outdoor feel. Maximising light and nature within are not just good for our well-being but are also nourishing for the soul.

Indoor gardening.

# Chapter 4

# Colour lover

*Your choice of colours sets your stage.*

Creating a stylish home becomes a whole lot easier if you have a basic understanding of how to use colour. Beware, there are whole books expertly dedicated to this enormous subject, so I will just share with you my approach and my passion for how to use it for that Relax Max look and feel.

Colour holds a tremendous emotional significance, and plays a pivotal role in shaping the way that a space feels. In a Relax Max home, where emotional context is paramount, painting a room is one of the most transformative things we can do. Our choice of colours for walls, furniture, and décor sets the stage and is essential for crafting our desired mood.

Each colour has the power to evoke specific feelings and emotions, imparting warmth or freshness, energy or peace, to our living spaces. For instance, pink has a nurturing, comforting vibe, whilst green is reminiscent of nature and growth. Likewise, muted colours and earthy tones provide a sense of cosiness and calm, in contrast to the vibrancy and enthusiasm of bold, bright hues. It's no surprise, then, that my seaside home is filled with a soothing palette that contains plenty of sludgy pinks and greens.

# Think colour palette, not coloured wall

When we think about using colour in our homes, we normally go straight to the colour we are going to paint our walls. This is understandable, because the walls are the biggest surface area in a room and so we think that's the right place to start. But walls aren't everything! They are just one part of our colourful home and shouldn't be thought of in isolation. So, don't begin by just thinking about the colour of the walls; instead, think about a colour *palette*. Your colour palette will inform the colour of the walls *and* help with colours for the rest of the room.

## What is a colour palette?

A colour palette for a room is essentially a thoughtfully curated selection of colours for you to use within a specific space. In interior design it usually includes about three colours—typically, one main colour, complemented by two supporting colours. When combined, these colours work harmoniously together and contribute to the overall atmosphere of the room.

Whilst I wouldn't want to dictate which colours are right for someone else's home, for a Relax Max style, I typically steer away from a palette filled with bright, zingy, sparkly, popping colours. Instead, I tend to favour a colour scheme that leans more towards those muted, earthy tones. Think subdued shades, like salmon-y pinks and moss greens, warm mustards, sludgy blues, or beautiful browns, mixed in with plenty of wood and neutrals. All complemented by a few corners in warm dark colours for cosiness. These are the colours I love, and they contribute to the calming atmosphere I try to cultivate. Incorporating those pops of brighter oranges, reds, deep pinks, or yellow as accents will grab a little bit of attention and inject some energy into a space.

---

Pinks and greens.

My colour palette. Subdued shades, natural neutrals, accents of pink, red, and yellow with floral patterns.

## 60:30:10 Rule

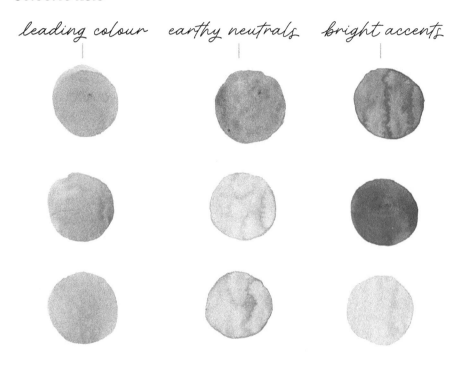

*leading colour   earthy neutrals   bright accents*

Pick your colour palette. A leading colour, a neutral, and an accent.

Once you have chosen the colours in your colour palette, you will need to decide how much of each colour to use in your room. In interior design, there's a really helpful guideline, known as the 60:30:10 rule, that gives you the basic ratios to work to.

It says that, in a palette of three colours, you should dedicate around 60 percent of the space to your main colour—this is the leading colour and is usually the colour on your walls.

Add in your secondary colour at about 30 percent. In my home it is always a neutral—reminiscent of natural elements such as stone or plants or wood. This colour is frequently the background to my floral sofas or the colours in the rugs or flooring.

Reserve approximately 10 percent for the last colour, the accent colour—these are the pops of colour which can be bolder and brighter because they are used so sparingly, often on things such as cushions or lamps.

Once you understand this principle, you won't ever look back—I promise. It's the key to achieving a balanced colour scheme in any room, and it's truly that straightforward. By limiting your palette and sticking to this type of ratio, you'll consistently create a well-coordinated and harmonious scheme. This approach will give you the confidence to incorporate those colourful accents, rich textures, and varied patterns.

As you experiment and grow more confident, you can then adapt this rule to suit your own style. If you want to add another colour or pattern, for example, add it in a small way—a cheeky extra 5 percent, just like my bedroom, can really make a room zing!

60 percent pink, 30 percent neutral,
10 percent yellow (plus a cheeky extra 5 percent red)

# Small accents, big impact

Accent colours are those delightful splashes of colour that can effortlessly elevate the look of a room. Despite their modest size, they wield considerable influence—so much so that they warrant an entire section to themselves! Accent colours can be introduced through something as simple as a vase of flowers, a piece of art, or a pattern on a cushion.

Moreover, these accents offer a fantastic way to transform the feel of a room without breaking the bank or investing hours of labour in permanent changes. With just a swift swap of your cushions or flowers, any room can undergo a five-minute facelift, adapting to the seasons or reflecting a particular mood.

Accents also excel at linking colour schemes across rooms, and even your whole home.

Flower facelift.

# Linking your accent colours

## Threads

Throughout this book, I keep coming back to the idea of weaving links throughout our homes, creating connections that help to bring about harmonious and unified spaces. Much like the recurring themes in a novel, these links contribute to a more cohesive whole by acting as a through-line, or connective thread, between individual elements and rooms.

Here, the links manifest as threads of colour, weaving through our living spaces and seamlessly connecting one room to another. For instance, yellow accents act as a unifying thread in my home. The kitchen is painted in a warm, burnt yellow, whilst a large painting with a mustard-yellow background has pride of place in a hallway. In the study, a bright yellow cushion sits on a floral sofa, and in a bedroom, a yellow checked blanket rests at the end of a bed. Whilst these subtle colour hints might well go unnoticed if you came to visit, what they do is create a subliminal link and sense of unity that flows throughout the entire house.

So, please think about adding some threads of colour to your home. Think of them as your hidden treasures—whilst they might not be obvious, they always create a pleasing subconscious connection!

Threads of yellow.

## Reflections

Another clever trick to have up your sleeve involves the power of colour reflection. It's quite similar to the concept of threads of colour, but with a twist: this time you're echoing your accent colours within the *same* room. Which means that, essentially, you want to reflect a colour from one area of the room to another. This technique works wonders in bringing a delightful sense of unity and cohesion to a space, ensuring that no colour feels isolated or disconnected.

For example, take this room: the red hue of the lamp cord is echoed in the poppies on the painting. Additionally, the pink of the sofa is reflected in the subtle pink of the tulips, while accents of green are scattered throughout. By reflecting the colours in this manner, you're able to establish a harmonious and cohesive atmosphere, seamlessly linking different elements within an eclectic or maximalist interior.

Red cord, red flowers.

# If you are stuck

**Choose a colourful focal point,** such as a piece of artwork, a rug, a random tile, or a piece of furniture, and build your palette around it.

**Take inspiration from nature,** as it offers a wide range of beautiful colour combinations. Greens and browns, blues and sandy beiges, or a sunset of pink and orange. There are endless possibilities.

**Always consider the mood or atmosphere** you want to create in your room. Warm colours like pinks and yellows will create a cosy and inviting atmosphere, while cooler tones like blues and greens will evoke a sense of calmness. And don't forget to think about the intended purpose of each room. Is it primarily a daytime space, calling for a light and airy feel? Or is it a night-time retreat, where a darker, cosier colour scheme might be nicer for cocooning?

**Utilise the resources of the top paint companies:** you can also tap into the resources offered by many paint companies. Begin by exploring their online platforms, where you'll discover pre-designed colour schemes and palette ideas. If you prefer a more hands-on approach, visit their stores, where knowledgeable staff can assist you in curating paint samples into cohesive schemes. For a personalised touch, consider engaging one of their colour consultants, who can provide tailored recommendations for a bespoke palette.

Turn to nature.

# White is also a colour!

White walls, colourful furniture.

Adding colour to your home is fantastic, and I obviously highly recommend painting your room if you haven't ventured into the world of colour before. I also understand that this could be a bit overwhelming, so if you are fond of your white walls, that's absolutely fine too! In our seaside house, the kitchen is in a dark basement, the floor, walls, and ceiling are all white, and the colours are introduced through furniture and accessories. If you want to add colour but are hesitant, start with the lightest blue or palest pink on your walls. If that is still too much, begin with colourful cushions, art, or rugs. Remember, the key to creating a Relax Max home is to choose a colour palette that resonates with you. It doesn't mean that every surface needs to be a colour statement.

# The power of your colour palette

Shifting your mindset into focussing on colour palettes, as opposed to individual colours, is super powerful and is a total game-changer. It really simplifies the decorating of a room, because you have a clear framework of colours to choose from that all work together. Your decision-making becomes a whole lot easier. With a colour palette decided, the groundwork for your colour choices is now done. Woohoo! So, whether you are choosing a paint colour for the wall, or a colour for a chair, or cushion, or lampshade or rug, if it fits into your colour palette, the chances are that it will work in your room.

I like to think of these colour palette benefits as the three Cs.

## The Three Cs

**Confidence.** Having a defined colour palette instils confidence in your decorating choices. Your options are narrowed down and guided by the chosen colours, making every decision a much smoother process—a welcome relief in my indecisive world!

**Cohesion**. Colour palettes play a pivotal role in establishing cohesion and unity within a Relax Max home. They connect the dots and establish links between eclectic choices of furniture and accessories. They ensure that all these elements sit together harmoniously—as opposed to sitting in cluttered chaos!

**Character.** Selecting a colour palette that resonates with you allows you to express your personal style. It's a reflection of your taste and character. Whether you adore bright and bold hues or prefer soft and muted tones, your chosen palette becomes a canvas for your unique preferences.

# Colour drenching

Once again, *the* most important thing when considering painting your room is to *not* just think about the wall colour—but for a different reason this time. It is far better to think, not *walls*, but *surfaces*. Walls are just some of a number of surfaces that frame a room. Forgetting about skirting boards, window frames, picture rails, and ceilings, and leaving them a bright white, is a huge "no" because you need them to work with your wall colour. They should be a part of your colour palette.

Imagine, for a moment, that you have carefully selected a beautiful green colour to paint the walls in your sitting room. You have scoured paint company websites and stores and tried endless samples to find it. You paint it solely on the walls and leave the rest of the woodwork a stark white. That white is jarring. It disrupts the harmony, and makes the room feel disjointed. Imagine, on the other hand, a different approach, where the same lovely green not only envelops the walls, but seamlessly flows across the woodwork and picture rails too.

Which is where colour drenching comes in. Colour drenching—despite being a trendy term right now—is a painting technique that has been in use for a considerable time. It involves applying a single paint colour to the walls, woodwork, window frames, and sometimes even the ceilings of a room. This approach is particularly well-suited to a Relax Max interior, as it effectively streamlines the overall appearance of your space, minimising the presence of distracting additional colours. This, in turn, allows the carefully curated patterns, textures, and furnishings to take centre stage. It's a simple yet effective trick that I use a lot because it is marvellous at creating that harmonious feeling I am constantly after.

And even if colour drenching isn't for you, don't leave your woodwork and ceilings that bright white! Choosing a colour for them that complements the wall colour, even if it is an off-white, will ensure that your room looks much more cohesive and considered.

Drenched green.

# Chapter 5

# Textured and patterned

*Patterns are the game-changer.*

## Tactile textures

When we refer to texture in interior decorating, we are talking about how something feels and what it looks like. Texture can be physical or visual. It can range from the rough and rugged feel of a jute rug to the smooth, silky appearance of a velvet sofa. Textures can vary from glossy to matte, shiny to dull, and come in an array of patterns and designs.

Texture adds a wonderful, sensory dimension to a space, but is one of those areas that are so often overlooked when decorating our homes.

---

Countless textures and patterns.

**Textures we commonly use**

**Natural textures**

- Wood
- Stone
- Woven materials like rattan or jute

**Soft and plush textures**

- Velvet
- Silk
- Knitted fabrics

**Shiny or reflective textures**

- Mirrored surfaces
- Polished surfaces
- Gloss paint

# Texture for atmosphere

Texture plays a pivotal role in shaping the atmosphere of a room, even at first glance. For example, imagine an industrial loft apartment. What can you see? I expect you have a mental image of the rugged textures of exposed brick walls, stone floors, sturdy steel beams, and ironwork. Completing this look might involve adding distressed leather furniture, rough linen cushions, and substantial rugs. There is an atmosphere of workmanship, of industry, of authentic times gone by.

In contrast, envision a cosy, autumnal reading nook. Can you see it? I see the softness of fluffy sheepskins and warm woollen blankets. It's layered with plush velvet cushions on sofas and accented by brushed brass candlesticks on tables. These textures create an inviting and snug atmosphere.

Both of these looks are achieved with just texture alone. Isn't it amazing how powerful it is?!

So, when we are talking about textures, we don't want to limit our thoughts to a few cushions on a bed. We're thinking about a holistic approach that encompasses these soft furnishings, but also includes flooring, walls, and hard surfaces. It's the interplay of these diverse elements that creates the intrigue and captivates the senses. Filling a room with varying textures offers possibilities of contrast, cosiness, and a touch of glamour all in one. It allows us to achieve a perfect blend of comfort and style in our living spaces. Without texture, a room can feel rather flat and uninspiring. With texture, it becomes a room in which we want to linger.

Just a splash of texture will do.

Adding texture does not mean choosing textures of any colour! When venturing into this textural world, it's essential to stay close to your well-defined colour palette—those few colours. This restraint sets the stage for that textured symphony you are about to create. It allows you to infuse your space with contrast and intrigue at every turn.

## Where to add texture

There is the opportunity for adding texture in many parts of a room. It's not just the texture of cushions and rugs. We can also add texture to the surfaces of the room: the floors, walls, ceilings. They serve as the framework or canvas for the entire space.

### Floors

To bring drama to your floors, think about the transformative power of rugs. Layering woollen rugs over shiny wooden or concrete surfaces is a simple yet highly effective choice. In my home, rugs are an essential feature in every room. Whether you are stacking them on top of each other for a stylish effect or even placing them on carpeted floors, rugs effortlessly infuse warmth and texture into the space.

Wicker and old wood textures.

### Walls and ceilings

You can even consider the surfaces of your ceilings. Ceilings can be painted or papered to add texture. My kitchen ceiling, for example, is painted in a high-gloss-textured finish so that it bounces the light around a dark and gloomy space. You can enhance plain walls by introducing decorative panelling or by revealing the rustic charm of exposed rough bricks. This works well in the bathroom or kitchen. These textured finishes bring depth and character to your living space.

### Soft furnishings

Instantly enhance any spot with the simplicity of textile layering. From throws and cushions on your sofa to the thoughtful layering of different kinds of bedding, you will swiftly infuse your room with cosiness. Don't settle for flat cushion covers or plain beds, either. Seek out hints of texture, like charming waffle-patterned cushions, tufted throws, or wafty curtains, and then style them with aplomb!

## Mixing and matching

Embrace the art of mixing and matching textures. Create contrast and interest by incorporating a variety of textures into your furniture and décor. Strive for a balance between flat and shiny, polished and tufted—think leather chairs and knitted blankets. This is how a room truly comes to life.

Brick texture and a small boat!

# Secret ingredient

Texture, therefore, is our secret ingredient in cultivating that inviting, laid-back and comfortable Relax Max atmosphere in a room. It brings warmth through soft throws and blankets, introduces contrast with earthy terracotta pots on top of shining coffee tables, or rugs on stone floors, and infuses life into spaces through fabric and pattern (see page 103). If you've remained guided by your colour palette, these textural layers will work harmoniously together to create that depth and interest, helping to define your personal style.

So, whether you're aiming to create a cosy autumnal corner or an industrial loft vibe, remember that textures hold a key to transforming your space. It's remarkable how much can be achieved with texture alone!

One scene, many textures.

**Top Tips for adding Texture**

Limit your colour palette

Add texture layer by layer, building depth and character

Mix and match your textures to create tension and captivate interest

# Perfect patterns

If there was just one thing I would urge you to incorporate into your decorating, it's some pattern.

You see, patterns are the game-changer when creating a truly inviting Relax Max interior. To me, a room without any pattern feels flat, a bit cold; there's a sense that something is missing. Add a touch of pattern to a corner and you add a bit of joy, warmth and playfulness. Patterns add that little bit of deliciousness to any spot. And here's the thing: pattern can do all of this whilst maintaining those relaxing, harmonious vibes.

There are, of course, instances where pattern takes centre stage, making a bold and loud statement that demands attention—but it doesn't have to be like that. By adhering to our restrained colour palette, or choosing a quiet pattern, we can ensure that patterns add interest to our rooms but don't dominate.

You can weave patterns through your space in so many ways: think cushions that "pop," floral sofas that steal the show, curtains that elegantly frame your windows, wallpapers that bring walls to life, and rugs that ground the room with their woven designs.

**Top Tip**

If you see a pattern you love—whether it's on a beautiful tile, cushion, wallpaper, or sofa—choose that first and then select your colour palette to complement it.

My sitting room colours were inspired by the fabric for my sofa—I painted the lightest of pinks on the walls, adding green through the plants. The brown and beige are picked up through the coffee table and rugs.

The accents change with the seasons.

A posy pattern. →

A blossoming sofa.

# Pattern partners

Whilst I will always appreciate a room with a patterned sofa, or rug or cushion, the true magic lies in incorporating multiple patterns into our spaces. That's what elevates the effect. It's the seamless blending of various patterns that helps to shape the unique character of a Relax Max home. The beauty is that you can mix numerous patterns in countless ways—whether it's pairing an eye-catching floral with an animal print, a delicate ditzy pattern with some stripes, or even combining all four!

But how do you achieve this? How do you create a pattern mix that seamlessly comes together, where each pattern complements the others, yet still maintains enough of a mismatched charm to spark interest?

The first step to achieving this mismatched harmony is to revisit the concept of colour threads. You need to find a thread of a single colour that runs through your patterns. This thread is what ties them together and avoids any sense of disconnect. This common colour will bring a sense of purpose and balance—setting your patterns up to blend seamlessly and coexist in perfect harmony!

You also want to consider the scale of the patterns that you are using. For example, you probably wouldn't want to pair two large, dominating patterns together, as this can be overwhelming. Instead, think about the mixing of opposites. Contrast a big pattern with a smaller, more delicate one. If you have a room with a large floral pattern, like I have on my sofa, introduce some thin stripes or a smaller floral design on a cushion to complement it. This contrast creates a lovely dynamic.

Incorporate some unexpected patterns into the mix as well. Unique motifs, such as a painting of a vase of flowers or a bird embroidered onto a cushion, can serve as subtle patterns. Think of these details as a clever way to introduce some pattern into a space without overwhelming it. This is a technique I frequently employ.

Now add some black or white or animal print to your pattern mix. It might surprise you, but these patterns can act as neutrals. Yes, you read that right! Animal print, with its timeless appeal, can function as a neutral base. So, consider incorporating a black-and-white striped cushion or a bit of leopard print to any pattern mix. They are fabulous for enhancing that look we are aiming for.

To prevent pattern overload, it's important to include some solid sections within your pattern mix. This means adding cushions or other accessories of a single colour. These solid elements act as anchors, grounding the mix of patterns, thereby preventing it from feeling chaotic. A simple way to do this is to choose a colour from one of your patterns and incorporate it as a single-coloured cushion.

## Top Tip
## The magic formula for perfect patterns

**Choose a base pattern** that sets the overall tone for the room. This might be wallpaper, a floral printed sofa, or a patterned rug. The base pattern serves as the foundation for the whole design.

**Consider the colour palette** and opt for patterns that share a common colour thread. This ensures that patterns work together seamlessly.

**Vary the scale** of your patterns to prevent them from competing with each other.

**Mix different styles**, such as stripes, florals, and gingham, and single colours to create the magic.

How many patterns can you see?

# Pattern for walls

Wallpaper is currently in fashion. It is making a huge comeback, having fluctuated in popularity over the years. To me, there are two distinct types: one is the dominating kind, with its bold designs and lots of colour. These wallpapers become the focal point of the room. Or there is the more subtle variety that adds interest without overwhelming. For maximalists who love bold designs, going all out on the walls can be marvellous. The alternative is wallpapers with classic designs in muted colours. They are quietly beautiful and create a stunning backdrop without overpowering the space. These wallpapers exude a timelessness and classic appeal, the kind of wallpaper that I wouldn't change until it literally fell off my walls!

Whether you have a bold wallpaper or a more muted one, you can still introduce other patterns into the room. Just make sure that you think about keeping the harmony with those threads of colour.

## Cloakrooms are a free hit!

A downstairs cloakroom is the ideal spot for daring wallpaper experimentation! These rooms are usually small, are often tucked away in dimly lit corners, and seldom receive a prolonged visit! Consequently, they serve as a perfect setting for embracing some bold patterns and out-of-your-comfort-zone design choices. Additionally, these small rooms often feature their own little foibles, such as a sloping ceiling, providing wonderful opportunities to experiment with things you wouldn't normally consider. Perhaps you could extend the wallpaper onto that quirky ceiling or add more adventurous ceiling colours. These rooms are the rooms in which to have fun.

In my own downstairs cloakroom, I've used a bold floral pattern that incorporates the various colours found throughout the rest of my home, including shades of pink, blue, and green. These colours link with the other colours in my house but are paired with a dark-coloured ceiling and woodwork. It creates an impact and yet sits comfortably within the house itself.

Floral patterned loo.

# For the love of floral sofas

I obviously can't talk about introducing pattern into a Relax Max home without talking about my favourite way to incorporate pattern into my home, a floral sofa!

At the last count, I had three floral sofas and two floral chairs! And I am sure that I will always find room for another one.

Floral sofas are where I fully embrace pattern. I don't have much wallpaper in my house, as my high ceilings make wallpaper a costly commitment. So floral sofas are my equivalent of wallpaper, and I absolutely, unequivocally love them. In the same way that there are two types of wallpaper, I feel that there are two types of floral sofa: those that are a bit bold and daring and those that serve as a more neutral backdrop. I have both.

## Why do I love them so much?

Mostly, I love floral sofas because I find them whimsical and carefree. They feel lighter and more interesting than traditional sofas of one colour. The latter can often appear as a big solid block of colour, potentially feeling heavy and overwhelming in a room. (My first foray into floral sofas coincided with the era dominated by all things grey, particularly sofas, none of which resonated with me.) It took months of dedicated hunting and endless searches in magazines and on Pinterest to find a sofa I loved—it was a floral one, and it really helped me to define my style.

If you are on the hunt for a floral sofa, choosing a floral pattern with a neutral background and muted colour palette will ensure versatility in your room. It allows the sofa to serve as a neutral component of a decorating scheme—surprisingly, in my opinion, they are much more neutral than the commitment to a single-coloured sofa, particularly if you have chosen one in a bold colour. You see, despite feeling like a riskier choice, floral sofas effortlessly complement various styles. One trick is to give a floral sofa a modern feel by upholstering a contemporary sofa in a traditional floral fabric, thus creating a striking contrast, and bringing their heritage into the twenty-first century.

Sunlit floral slumber.

I am also drawn to floral sofas because of the emotions they stir within me. Their delicate designs transport me to a bygone era with motifs of flowers, vines, and leaves evoking images of tranquil gardens and simpler times. The nostalgia tied to their historical popularity reminds me of the cosy, welcoming homes of grandparents or scenes from period films and literature. Their soft, whimsical patterns embody cosiness, creating a comforting atmosphere that harks back to a time when life felt slower. So, consider trying one for yourself—look for a modern one in a vintage-style fabric. I think you will love it!

# Chapter 6

# Life-affirming lighting

*Layering creates glowing, radiant pools of light*

First of all, please banish any thoughts of solitary light bulbs, dangling in small shades from the centre of a ceiling, as the primary source of lighting for a room. These lights cast a stark, uninviting glow across a room at all times of day and should be removed from your mind!

Imagine, instead, a home where magical lighting draws you into its cosy spots. There's a strategically positioned chair that catches the early morning sunbeams; just perfect for the first cup of tea of the day. There's a sofa, bathed in the gentle, dappled light of the afternoon sun. As daylight wanes, there are comforting pools of gentle light cast by the decorative lamps that grace the rooms at dusk.

How do we feel when we imagine the above? For me, it's that comforting, magical feeling that beautifully lit rooms have the power to imbue. We all know that light profoundly influences our emotions, and I believe that, regardless of the day we may have had, it is very uplifting to return home to warmly lit spaces and corners. So, whether we're making the most of sunlit nooks or decorating our space with lively layers of lamps, getting the lighting right gives us a comfortably warm and inviting room. And the key to this is to include much more light in your room than you could possibly first imagine.

Sofa in sunshine.

# Lighting inside and out

It would be understandable to interpret *lighting* as the lights that we put inside our homes, the lights that are powered by electricity. For me, this is only half the story. It is important to remember that the lighting in any room comes from both the inside *and* outside. So, I think we need to think of lighting much more holistically. We must include the light *we* put into the room *and* the light that naturally comes into the room from the *outside*. It's important to manage, design, and blend the influence of the two. That's the Relax Max way to think.

# Lighting is dynamic

Again, we could be forgiven for thinking that lighting is binary—it's either turned on or turned off—painting a static picture of a lit or unlit room. However, the reality is far more dynamic.

The truth is that the light in a room changes throughout the day, across the seasons, and with the weather! The cold harsh light of a grey day in winter is very different to the golden light of a summer's afternoon. And, as morning turns to evening, so the natural light streaming into our room transforms with the passing hours. Likewise, the room's purpose and the way we use it also fluctuate. So, the lights we have should be flexible and changeful. Fortunately, there are endless lamps and lighting choices that can be employed at different times of the day for different kinds of moods, occasions, and functions. If you need a bright light for cooking, which later turns into subdued lighting for a cosy evening supper with friends, there's an option for it all, and in the same spot.

It is important to think of lighting as a "movable feast," as a flexible set of illuminations and atmospheric nuances that can change a mood, set an ambience, and help to define spaces. Why settle for bad lighting when the beautiful options are endless?!

Pools of light.

# Daylighting

Natural daylight is a natural mood enhancer, so finding the best spots in our homes to take advantage of this magical elixir is a must. Ensuring that furniture is positioned to maximise its benefits might seem obvious, but it is often overlooked.

So, take a moment to survey your home and recognise these sunny spots as *features*. In our home, the most cherished spots are always on our sofas, nestled in front of our windows. They bask in the best of the sunshine at any time of the year; there's always someone on one, including a dog, who has usually claimed the most coveted spot! Likewise, if you frequently work from home, you may want to consider placing your desk near a window— you get not only the best of the natural light whilst working but also the view to the outdoors to inspire you.

# Layers of lights

Lighting is marvellous for adding shadows and contrast to a room, and for drawing our attention to specific areas. A mix of lighting sources achieves this effect, whereas a single overhead light cannot. Those lone light bulbs can't light up a dark corner or show off a painting, and they don't encourage our eyes to linger.

You see, lighting is collaborative. It's about creating as many beautiful glowing pools of light as you can. So, consider placing three or four smaller lamps with lower-wattage bulbs strategically around your space. Place them at varied heights and levels to add depth and warmth to any room. Pop table lamps on coffee tables or behind sofas. Place a floor lamp next to an armchair, add a desk lamp to a desk, and don't forget to add candles or fairy lights for that evening atmosphere. Be generous with your lighting; you will never have too many little lights—but it is easy to have too few!

---

Dogs tell you where the sunny spots are.

Layer your lights at different heights.

Now let's think about the beauty of all these different lights and how to use them.

## Hanging lighting (the top layer)

So far, I have given ceiling lights a bad press. As I might have mentioned, I am not a fan of those single bulbs hanging all alone in the centre of the room! However, when used skilfully, hanging lights are fabulous.

Firstly, you need to move them away from the centre of a room and be creative with the height at which they are hung. Then they become marvellous at defining specific areas within a space and for providing a sense of focus to that area. Low hanging shades sitting over dining tables, bedside tables, or kitchen islands are particularly good at this. You can also consider clustering two or three pendant lights together. Whether hung in a straight line over an island, or grouped as a trio over that dining table, these lights seamlessly blend style and function.

Next, consider the type of hanging light, because there are many sorts and they come in an array of materials. There are glass chandeliers, lanterns made of paper, pendant lights in beaten metal, and shades made from wicker or fabric, to name but a few. Their finest incarnations manipulate light and create a mesmerising atmosphere.

If you do find yourself with a lone bulb suspended from the ceiling, perhaps in a rental space or a hallway, consider making a bold statement with the shade. Go big and beautiful, choosing a shade that elegantly diffuses the light, adding that touch of enchantment.

Get the position and shade right, make sure they are dimmable, and hanging lights become a feature as opposed to a horror!

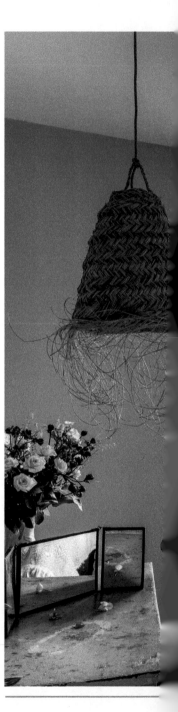

**Top Tips**

- Do choose warm light bulbs, as opposed to cool ones, if you want to create that softer, more flattering feel.
- Do install dimmer switches to adjust the brightness as needed, allowing you to set the perfect mood for any occasion.

Low hanging ceiling lights define the areas of this small bedroom.

## Floor lamps (the middle layer)

Introducing floor lamps into our rooms creates an additional layer of lighting. Their position, spanning the space between the ceiling and the table, injects an extra layer of height into the spots we place them. This helps to bring a lively rhythm of lighting into a room, drawing our eyes in, around, and up, encouraging us to keep looking.

Popped next to a sofa or chair in the sitting room, they are ideal for reading, lighting up the spots where we curl up with a book. In the bedroom, they can make fabulous alternatives to bedside lamps, and their glowing pools of light are super effective for brightening up dark corners or challenging spaces.

There are so many shapes and sizes available, and those that are equipped with dimmers allow us to change the mood with ease—bright for reading, dim for welcoming. Whether standing tall in a corner, or arching gracefully over a sofa, floor lamps are an often-overlooked addition to a space.

## Table lamps (the bottom layer)

There is something special about table lamps. The beautiful pools of light they create are always mood-enhancing, but they also make the most wonderful decorating tools. In fact, there is barely a table in my house without a table lamp. I particularly love them on coffee tables, big and small. Sometimes I have been known to buy a table in order to place a beautiful table lamp on top of it! Like floor lamps, table lamps light up gloomy corners. They are welcoming in a hallway and look beautiful on a dressing table, reflected in a mirror. I often have them on kitchen counters, windowsills, and dressers for that added touch of cosiness.

Floor lamps can make a corner.

Lighting up a
dark hallway.

### Rechargeable table lamps

These are a relatively new idea and they have literally revolutionised our lighting possibilities. They make it possible to light up those all those challenging spots where access to a plug socket is limited or not feasible. No longer constrained by trailing cables around rooms or beneath rugs, you can now have little lamps in front of a sofa, or on a bookcase. You can even put them in bathrooms, where traditional electric outlets are unsafe. These little table lamps have given us the freedom to place lights wherever we want, bringing those enchanting pools of light to any spot imaginable.

# Lampshades

Lampshades are the "outfits for our lamps." I have more lampshades than I have lamps, and I change some of my lampshades with the seasons or simply because I feel like a change. It's a really simple way to change up your décor. In my Relax Max, pattern-loving home, I have a whole host of shades made from beautiful fabrics with a decorative feel. When lit up, they create a beautiful glow, yet when the light is off, these shades are still a part of my decoration, partners to the other fabrics and patterns in the room.

## Mix or match, or not!

First, you need to decide whether you would prefer a coordinated set of lampshades or a mix-and-match approach to your room. While I typically opt for mixing lamp styles, there are instances where uniformity can make a stronger statement. For example, matching lamps over a kitchen island or table is always striking. Similarly, bedside lamps can either match, or just complement each other. This will depend on the style of the lamp and the look you are after. And remember, even if you choose to have a pair of matching lamps in a room, there will always be room for a few others that can mix in and create the more laid-back look.

So, assuming that we aren't going for that perfectly matched look, how do we ensure coherence whilst mixing lamp styles?

Firstly, we want them to have at least one thing in common: for example, a colour. You could have two or three different patterned lamps in the room if they share a common colour to link them together. Or you can mix up the textures of lamps—wicker, beaded, glass—but keep them all in a gorgeous natural colour to keep that continuity.

Alternatively, you can create the same harmony by selecting lampshades from the same collection or series. For example, the shades below are all different, but they sit happily together because they share a common theme.

Ultimately, the goal is to find a unifying element amongst your lamps—be it colour or size or pattern or texture!

# Decorative lights

Fairy lights and candles aren't just for Christmas! A sprinkling of decorative lighting around a room adds that something extra. Nothing beats the twinkle of a fairy light or the flickering of a candle at any time of the year.

Lampshades are outfits for lam

# Chapter 7

# Things to make you smile

*Adding a hint of disruption elevates*

*a room's appeal.*

If you search on Google for "things you need for a house," it reveals many lists like, "The 100 Essential Household Items Everyone Should Have." Each list includes everything from toilet seats to built-in paper towel holders: all the practical, rational items that make a house functional. But when I consider what is essential in a home, I would never think this way.

As ever with Relaxed Maximalism, my list of "things you need for a house" would take a much more emotional perspective. It includes things that make a house feel like a cosy home: the items that add warmth and personality to a space, the things we surround ourselves with, not out of necessity, but because they make us happy.

So, whether you're renting your first-ever flat or setting up your forever home, these other things do matter. What follows is my list, which includes my personal essentials. Some of them you may already have; others, you can find with just a little searching, and a few are worth saving up for.

Just add a chicken!

# Page-turning décor

Books are quite possibly my favourite decorative items in a home. They are scattered throughout my living space; I have them everywhere. My shelves are full to bursting with books I have read and loved. Books that I intend to read are piled high in teetering towers by my bed! I have coffee-table books on coffee tables, and there are the novels that decorate my windowsills.

Every book holds some significance for me. Often, they are a reminder of the time and place where I found myself caught up in in the story. *American Wife* takes me back to the windy beach in Portugal where I read for two solid days. Or there are the countless page-turning thrillers that provided much-needed escapism during the Covid lockdown at home in 2020. My overflowing bookshelves remind me of authors I once loved but have forgotten. Other books hold sentimental value, connecting me to the person who gave them to me—*Any Human Heart*, from my dad, *The Time Traveller's Wife*, from my mum.

Our books are full of endless possibilities and meaning, offering glimpses of who we are or perhaps who we aspire to be. And whilst we may not buy as many physical books as we used to, with paperbacks transitioning to e-readers and encyclopaedias finding their home on Google, they remain beautiful objects reflecting our passions and interests.

So I don't think of books only as something to read, but also as symbolic of the person who owns them. Their very presence brings personality and warmth to a space, infusing it with a sense of the person who lives there.

A pile of books can
be simply beautiful.

It's hard to find a surface that isn't improved by a stack of books, piled high
on a bedside table, or even the floor. But, no matter where they are, books
look best when you think about how to style them. Sometimes you might
use a book or three to help with the spot you are styling—adding a feature
to a coffee table, for example, or some height to a shelf. At other times, you
may be decorating a bookshelf, or creating a book nook, like mine.

# Bookshelf style

Books have had a very clear convention about how they are displayed. They are placed upright, in rows, on dedicated bookshelves, with the spines facing out. I have hundreds of books in my house, and almost none are displayed exactly like that! You see, there are many ways to present your books. You can still organise them alphabetically by author or by topic, but now we see a lot more books organised by colour or even with the spines facing in. Whichever way you are doing it, books look better when they are styled with a mix of objects.

**Styling your bookshelf**

Think small. Style your bookshelf by arranging small clusters of books—group a few books at a time, rather than in one continuous row.

Vary the height. Place some books in vertical rows, next to others in horizontal stacks.

Break up the rhythm. Place an ornament on top of a low pile of books. Add a vase, plant, or sculpture to an empty space.

Layer up. Hang pictures in front of the shelves to create depth.

Make it glow. Frame your bookshelf with fairy lights, or leave a spot for a little lamp.

Bookshelves are more than
just shelves for books!

# A cosy book nook

If you can find a spot in your home to create a little book nook, it adds a really comforting feel, and you can make one literally anywhere. If there's a blank wall or a corner of a room you don't quite know what to do with, why not turn it into a book nook? It's actually quite straightforward.

Dedicate a wall to the bookshelf. Organise as on page 135. To ensure comfort, add a cosy chair, complete with a soft cushion and snuggly blanket, of course! You can add a footstool, if you have the space. A small side table, within arm's reach of your chair, is a must for resting your current book and a warm drink. To bring a touch of nature, add a vase of flowers to the side table. Complete the look with a lamp, to ensure that you have ample light for reading long into the night.

With these simple steps, you've created an inviting spot where you can immerse yourself in the pages of your favourite book, offering the perfect escape at home. Alternatively, you can simply add some books to a cosy corner and dub it your very own "book nook." Sometimes, simply assigning a name to a space can make it feel cosier and more defined!

Making a book nook.

# A collection or two

I like to think of our homes as "grand collections." They serve as the gathering place for all the things we both need and love. Once we have defined our style, everything we introduce blends seamlessly into this big collection we call "home." In essence, our Relax Max homes are thoughtfully curated collections that showcase our meaningful items, our personalities, and our life stories.

This perspective also brings order to the potential chaos of creating a beautiful home, because we ourselves are the thread that connects these carefully gathered possessions. Having smaller collections within this overarching "home collection" is equally delightful. These mini collections become integral parts of the whole, weaving additional threads into the tapestry of where we live.

Creating and displaying these smaller collections is undeniably a joy. It's also a simple, yet effective, way to transform an ordinary shelf into something marvellous. Collections, by their nature, are inherently unique; no one else will put together the exact same collection or display it in precisely the same way. There are countless items to collect, of course, but if you are unsure where to start, collecting for the kitchen is a simple starting point.

Put collections on a shelf.

# Collections to dine for!

Hunt for vintage tableware on which to serve your food...or tea! Choose it by colour or theme. You could look for plates in all the shades of blue, or bowls decorated only with strawberries or lemons. If you begin a search for vintage serving platters decorated with vegetables or fruit, as I did, you head down the most glorious rabbit hole! Glasses are another easy way to build a collection: old French ones with colourful stems in pink and green inject a touch of colour into any shelf display. Play with scale, mixing and matching heights, keeping it cohesive through colour or theme. Whether stacked on a shelf or laid on the table for dinner, these pieces will elevate the everyday to an occasion.

Wallplatter!

# The perfect vase?

Style your vases.

Gathering an array of vases is another straightforward launchpad into collecting. The beauty of collecting vases is that, no matter how many you possess, there never seems to be the perfect one for your current flowers! While finding the "one" may be an impossible quest, it does justify having a shelf brimming with many varied shapes and styles! Little cut-glass vases designed for a flower or two are perfect for bedside tables. Mantel vases add a touch of elegance to any collection and are excellent for displaying big-headed blooms like hydrangeas, whilst jugs of seasonal flowers always look lovely in the centre of a table and vintage pots and pans are marvellous for growing bulbs. Keep an eye out for vases with slender necks; they make arranging a small bunch a breeze. Those big ones with wide brims call for big bouquets, often at great expense!

## Tiny collections

You might want to collect items that are small, like pebbles and shells, rather than large items like vases. Finding a way to display these kinds of collections is essential for achieving a stylish rather than a cluttered look! I've found a perfect solution is to use vintage letterpress drawers, originally designed to organise small printing letters. They make beautiful containers for exhibiting those tiny treasures and collections that might otherwise remain hidden in a drawer. Whether it's matchbox cars and miniature animals, thimbles and buttons, or jewellery and antique keys, these drawers always make a beautiful display. Pop one on a shelf or hang it on the wall to create your own piece of art.

## Hero pieces

Every room deserves a hero piece of furniture. It's the item that pulls everything together and anchors the room in your style. It may be a piece of contemporary design or a timeless antique, but when you have one, it becomes the focal point of your room.

Having a hero stops a room from feeling bitty. I like to think of them as the main character in the story or the leading actor in a play. Not every cast member can play a leading role, but every story does need at least one strong character. In my library room, the lead "actor" is my bookcase; in my sitting room, it's my floral sofa; and in my study, it's the eighteenth-century dining table that I use as an extra desk.

These are the items that draw your eye in, command attention, and hold your gaze, giving substance to your décor. Whether it's a huge mirror, an oversized table lamp, a beautiful antique chest, or a large vintage rug, they are the items that are worth searching for. Having at least one in a room is essential, having two is a luxury, but more than three is probably too many!

Replace the letters with your collections.

## Big and Bold

Don't shy away from buying something oversized. Oversized pieces inject a dose of interest and intrigue into a space; they introduce a touch of off-balance charm and add a hint of disruption that elevates the room's appeal. Even in a smaller room, big pieces can add a sense of grandeur to a space.

In this small bedroom, antique French shutters serve as an enormous headboard, diverting attention from the super-king-size bed that might otherwise dominate the space. This oversized headboard is balanced by the large pendant lights that hang next to the bed. The result? A small room with a substantial bed that feels more spacious than its actual dimensions.

## Rugs

Rugs hold a special place in my heart; I have them practically everywhere, sharing the spotlight with those floral sofas. Vintage Moroccan rugs skim most of my floors, united by common colours and styles. Runners, perfect for narrow spaces, grace my kitchen floor, while carefully positioned rugs anchor tables in the heart of a room—my zebra-patterned rug works hard in my study. Animal print rugs effortlessly blend into any room, acting as neutrals to complement various patterns. When it comes to rugs, I always opt for the largest size possible, naturally!

## Antiques

I have been collecting antique pieces for a long time now. I don't have many, but those I do have, I love. When we lived in Singapore, I saved up for months to buy an old Chinese medicine chest. It then took many more months to find one that I could afford. This chest boasts around fifty tiny drawers, each divided into even smaller sections. To this day, I haven't put anything of value inside it, fearing that I will never find it again amongst the myriad of compartments! I also have a nineteenth-century green velvet chair, passed down from my parents and a worn, old dresser that I bought at auction. In almost every one of my rooms, you can find at least one antique piece that I have searched high and low to find.

These antiques ground a room with a sense of timelessness and a touch of old-world grandeur. You can feel their history in both their craftsmanship and their stories. If you are fortunate enough to inherit one, or you stumble upon a hidden gem in your grandmother's attic, consider yourself lucky. Otherwise, these might be the pieces that it is worth saving up for. Frequently these old treasures cost less than designer pieces of today, so they are definitely worth the hunt. You can find them at auction houses, vintage fairs, and antique shops aplenty. Nowadays there are lots of small independent sellers online; they strike a balance between thrift stores and high-end boutiques, streamlining the search for that ideal piece as they have done the legwork for you.

I saved long and hard for this medicine chest! See it with my zebra print rug and antique table.

# Art

In my home you will find lots of paintings and pieces of art, yet surprisingly, not many of them are hung on walls! Instead, I have pieces propped on floors and shelves, mantelpieces and windowsills. Some are hung on bookshelves, whilst one sits on the lowest panel of my staircase. I love to have art in unexpected places or at an unexpected height.

I found my favourite painting when we were travelling in Vietnam over one New Year. It's a silhouette of a girl with a long plait and I fell in love with the sense of peace she brought. We wouldn't usually have been able to afford her, but we managed to strike a New Year's bargain with the gallery owner. The rest of my art is mostly vintage, and found in all my usual places—eBay, charity shops, or antique centres. I love vintage pieces of art for the atmosphere they add, and there are some wonderful online sellers who can find some beautiful pieces for not too much.

I have never been a fan of gallery walls, despite their current trendiness. Instead, I tend to opt for a single piece that stands on its own and makes a statement. You can find reasonably priced big prints at online poster stores; they have a fabulous range. Look for the largest size they have, and let them frame it for you. A big picture brings a more substantial and expensive feel to a room, and I prefer this to having many small prints clustered together to fill the same amount of space.

Hero art.

# Chapter 8

# Secret Styling—shh!

*Our homes are thoughtfully curated collections that showcase our personalities and our life stories.*

Let's assume that you have chosen a room you want to style. You have got to grips with its layout, pinpointed the spots for those big-ticket items like sofas, beds, and kitchen tables. You've settled on your chosen colour scheme, drawn inspiration from your Pinterest boards and collected a few accessories. Now it's time to shift your focus to the styling—and how to bring everything together creatively and beautifully in one cohesive space.

So, lets touch on a few of my favourite Relax Max styling secrets that you can apply to every nook and cranny of your home. Whether you are revamping your sitting room, bedroom, bathroom or even just a kitchen shelf or window sill, these tips will help to ensure that every spot exudes effortless cool.

---

Floral harmony across rooms.

# Think in layers

Layers are one of the most important components of a Relax Max home. Simply put, every element in your space—be it your furniture, accessories, lights, or the patterns and textures you choose—is an individual layer. These layers, when artfully combined, create that touch of magic and add that depth and character to a room. Texture and pattern add interest, layers of light bring atmosphere, and layers of objects on tables and shelves weave style out of clutter. Colour serves as the foundational thread, ensuring that all of our layers are harmoniously working together.

The more layers a room has, the more interesting it will be. Layers infuse a room with a sense of discovery; they add hidden depths and nestle together to give rooms a sense of playful mystery. Layers can be peeled back and personalities are revealed. In a room with lots of layers, there is always more to uncover than is initially apparent. You never get tired of living in rooms like these.

So, when styling your room, it's crucial to think in these layers, gradually adding each element until it all blends harmoniously together, creating a space that is more than just the sum of its parts. To illustrate, let's consider a baking analogy.

A rug, a blanket, a book, and an elephant.

# Layer cake

Layering a room is like layering a cake.

You can think of building up the layers in a room like you build up the layers of a Victoria sponge cake.

You begin with a single layer of sponge, adding a layer of jam and a layer of cream, then another layer of sponge, and repeat the process to construct a multi-layered cake. Whilst each individual layer might be quite appetising on its own, it is the inclusion of the many layers that creates a more delicious whole. Without layers, the cake would just be very plain.

That's how you need to think about decorating a room, just like making a Victoria sponge—layer by layer. Spread layers of pattern across a sofa, lay textured rugs over the floor, place lights at varying heights throughout the room, and add layers of objects to shelves. Think in terms of levels and how they work together, just like your cake. And let your colour palette act as the flavour that ties it all together.

You will quickly discover that adding these layers to a room brings richness, personality, and depth. It creates unexpected links between things, lovely transitions across a space, and a sense of harmony through the variety.

I am not much of a baker, mainly because I'm not very good at it! So, this is my go-to cake that comes out for high days, holidays, and birthdays. Looking back on my childhood, it reminds me of hazy afternoons in late summer—in the garden with cake, tea, friends, a gentle breeze, and a sleeping dog—when the strawberries and raspberries were in season. Now, of course, berries are available all year round, and we can have this cake on Christmas day if we would like to! The secret to it is the extra layer of sweet and sticky finger-licking sauce that goes on top.

Just a heads-up—this is a back-of-an-envelope recipe, where the quantities for the filling and topping are flexible and really depend on personal preference!

# Sunny Strawberry Sponge Cake

*Cake*

200 g each of very soft butter,
self-raising flour, and caster sugar
4 eggs, beaten
1 tsp baking powder
2 tbsps milk

*Filling and topping*

jam of choice (ours is raspberry)
a punnet of strawberries and a punnet of raspberries
a carton of double cream
2 tbsp icing sugar

Mix together the cake ingredients, adding the milk last. Split the batter into two cake tins and bake at 180°C for about 20 minutes.

Whilst it is baking, whip the double cream with a big spoonful of icing sugar. Squish a few of the raspberries and chop the strawberries into bite-size pieces.

Once the cakes are cooked, let them cool. Spread one layer with your jam, then add dollops of whipped cream, those squished raspberries, and some of the strawberries. Put the other sponge on top.

Take a handful of the raspberries and a handful of the strawberries, mix them with a spoonful of icing sugar, and blitz them into a sauce. Push this mixture through a sieve and save it until you are ready to eat.

Top the cake with the remaining cream and berries (not the sauce yet).

Once you are ready to serve, make a pot of tea, pour the sauce over the whole lot, and enjoy!

# Divide and conquer

When faced with the task of styling an entire room, it can seem somewhat overwhelming. A simple strategy to make this feel more manageable is to begin by taking one small step—just like you do when you tackle any big project or long journey. Here, this means that you break your room down into small sections and then focus on just one of these sections at a time. This is a whole lot easier than attempting to style the whole room at once.

If you have already done all your background work, especially with your colour palette, you will find that by tackling one corner, one sofa, one bookshelf at a time, you'll slowly piece together a room that evolves with cohesion and harmony. Accent colours will reflect, textures will contrast, patterns will blend through the things they share. Remember, it doesn't need to be perfect right away, because the joy is in the journey, and you will love your room just that little bit more with each addition and each refinement.

Start with a small corner or nook.

# Small and medium and large!

When styling our rooms, it's essential to avoid filling them with items that are uniform in size and scale. Too much similarity in size can make a room feel somewhat flat. Instead, shake things up by varying the scale of one or two of your décor pieces to add that extra dimension.

Try grouping together items of different heights—tall, medium, and short—to create visual interest. Incorporating a floor lamp is also an excellent way to introduce some varied height to a space. Better yet, consider adding something oversized—remember "Big and Bold" from the last chapter?! Whether it's a large painting commanding attention on an empty wall, or a statement pendant light, these larger-than-life elements instantly infuse your room with drama and excitement.

Group some tall, medium, and
short things together, and add a book!

# Add some imperfection

Creating a Relax Max room that strikes the balance between carefree and messy can be surprisingly tricky! How do you create a space that feels relaxed and yet still maintains a sense of order? A room that looks like it is both liveable and beautiful?

One way is to strive for that casual vibe whilst retaining a hefty dose of tidiness. Start by arranging your furniture in a neat and organised manner. Then, deliberately, introduce a hint of imperfection. For instance, arrange your sofa cushions perfectly and then intentionally knock one off balance or add an odd one out. If you prefer a casually styled throw, drape it across the corner of your bed or sofa, rather than neatly folding it on the arms. Then adjust and tweak until you achieve the desired look.

When styling a bookcase, arrange everything to your liking and then introduce an intentional element of disarray. Remove a book, tilt another to one side, or deliberately make a picture slightly crooked. I do this with my windowsills too.

However, remember that starting with some semblance of order in your space is crucial to avoid it looking like a complete mess. It is the adding of those little, unexpected touches of casualness that infuses your room with that effortless charm.

---

Create some order and then mess it up a bit!

Asymmetrical
bedside tables.

## Asymmetrical style

Let's revisit the notion that our rooms need structure to avoid appearing chaotic, but we don't want to overdo that structure and make them feel too formal! Striking the right balance here is essential. In my experience, symmetry and asymmetry play pivotal roles in achieving this. Symmetry brings a sense of order and harmony to a room. However, too much symmetry can result in a rigid and stiff atmosphere, reminiscent of those overly formal sitting rooms where everything matches perfectly—sofas with matching cushions, flanked by identical tables topped with identical lamps!

In a Relax Max home, the goal is to create balance whilst maintaining informality. This is where asymmetrical styling comes into play. It involves balancing a room through similarity, but without creating sameness. Side tables on either side of a sofa or bed are excellent examples of how asymmetrical styling can work wonders. Whilst they don't need to match exactly, they don't want to look so different that they create discord. In asymmetrical styling, these tables can differ, but must share at least one common characteristic—be it shape, material, texture, or height—in order to bring that harmony.

Take, for example, my bedside tables. They share many similarities—they boast a similar shape and height, and both are crafted from wood. However, that is where the similarities end. They convey the message, "We resemble each other, but we aren't identical twins."

## A final note; just start!

When it comes to styling your rooms, I cannot say strongly enough that you should not let hesitation or indecision hold you back; just start! Follow your heart, and don't be afraid to experiment.

Mistakes happen; things might not quite work or look perfect the first time. Some things might not turn out exactly as you expected. But that's okay! It means you will have learned something that you wouldn't have learned if you hadn't started! If something hasn't immediately worked out, then take another look and rearrange. Have fun and infuse your rooms with your unique personality and style. Take pleasure in the process.

# Chapter 9

# Sitting rooms for sitting

*Give the room a feeling of visual richness*

Which room comes to mind first when you think of your home? For me, it is that relaxed communal space, mostly known as the sitting room (or lounge, or living room). Whatever name we use, it has the same meaning and feeling for us all.

When I picture myself coming back after a long day at work, or returning from a holiday, it is the sitting room space that I see myself in. There is something about that room that means "home" more than any other.

It's certainly the place where everything I love about home comes together. It's a space to sit back in, to dive into a book, to swap stories with a friend over a cup of tea, or to gather as a family for a movie night. It is a room to relax in, and yet it is also a social hub, where we spend quality time and guests can be entertained.

So, our living rooms are tasked with fulfilling a host of roles: we want a room which is comfortable enough to crash out in with a book or a movie, and yet it also needs to be versatile enough to entertain a friend or two. We want it to show our personality, and we want it to be our "wow" room too...but not too wow, making it too precious to live in!

---

Sitting rooms that you love to sit in!

Let's delve into the details of crafting this ideal space—a room that isn't just visually captivating and a reflection of our personalities, but is also functional, embracing comfort and practicality.

## Work those layers

In the previous chapter I talked about the concept of layering. The sitting room—with its furniture, textiles, and accessories—offers the biggest opportunity to put your layering skills to work. There are endless possibilities for adding layer upon layer of depth and interest.

There are some easy things to do here which are effective. Putting a coffee table in front of a sofa adds a layer. Placing a small lamp on a little table adds a layer too, as does simply layering a couple of different kinds of blankets on the arm of a chair.

## Mix-match the room

The sitting room also offers a fabulous opportunity for creative mixing and matching in your styling. Consider the various dimensions you could cross. Are you going through the decades by combining a contemporary sofa with an antique table? Are you cutting across geographies by placing an English armchair on a beautiful Moroccan rug? Maybe you are pairing casual items, like a fun ornament, with a formal piece, like a traditional candlestick. Or perhaps you are mixing some tea lights with a sparkly chandelier.

And it's not just about mixing and matching *things*. It's also about incorporating those differing patterns and textures—think of those cushions, rugs, and sofas. Have faith that these combinations can happily sit together in a Relax Max sitting room, capturing our gaze and inviting us to appreciate the delightful contrasts you've curated. It's this mixing and matching that imbues the room with a sense of visual richness that unfolds before our eyes.

Mix-match living!

# Design for sitting

It's important not to forget that there is a very important functional requirement of a sitting room. Sitting!

It's no coincidence that the room in which you sit down the most is called the sitting room! (For those who call it the lounge, it's still the place in which you lounge the most!) Whatever you call it, the clue is in the name.

Whilst we spend most of our time seated in our sitting rooms, it's worth remembering that sitting down doesn't just mean one thing.

Everyone has their go-to sitting position: sat up, sat down, feet up, feet down, leant back, lying back, even just flopped. Plus, the dog must join in somewhere too! It also depends upon what we are doing at the time. If we are having a conversation, we want to be sat up, close enough to chat. Watching TV is more of a lean-back experience. Browsing on a laptop computer needs a little more support. Reading a book or scrolling on a phone means we curl up with a pile of cushions. For forty winks, we need to just rest our heads.

Ensuring flexibility and versatility in the seating arrangement of your sitting groom is crucial for ensuring everyone feels comfortable. So, try to exploit varying kinds of seating to provide options. In addition, be generous with the cushions, bolsters, and blankets. In our house, we each have our own favourite cushion/blanket combinations! And I am not exaggerating when I say that Twiglet does too!

Always space for a dog to sit too!

# The chairs

Whilst writing this chapter, it dawned on me that we often take these pieces of furniture for granted, but I think they deserve some appreciation! It's important to remind ourselves of how we use these seats, and how we fit them into our sitting rooms in a Relax Max manner.

## Sofas

The sofa is *the* spot to sink into at the end of a tiring day, so make sure it has the comfort you need. Try not to buy a sofa you haven't sat on first.

It will also be the biggest piece of furniture in the room, so it is important to make it a beautiful centrepiece, not a dominant eyesore! I usually choose my floral sofas, as I think they guarantee a lovely style. However, it's the accessories, both on and around the sofa, that will make your Relax Max room.

Layer those cushions on the sofa with their mixed fabrics and contrasting textures and patterns. I find the best way to style my cushions is to group them together at either end of the sofa—this seems to avoid that overwhelming look.

Equally, adding throws to a sofa enhances not only our warmth and comfort, but also the look and feel of the sofa. Throws are also an easy way to add a pop of accent colour or another pattern, giving a softness to the design as well as the touch. I have at least one on every sofa, and sometimes there are even three. Layer some neatly over the arm, or drape one stylishly across the seat.

Sofa corner.

# Armchairs

When I think of armchairs, I always picture the living room at my in-laws' house. It's a large room, so they do have the luxury of plenty of space, and whilst the décor might not exactly match my style, they have totally nailed the whole comfortable-seating thing. Each of my in-laws has a huge squishy green leather armchair to themselves. And when I say "squishy," I mean that you literally sink into it. Both chairs somehow manage to face both the TV and another sofa for conversational ease—with my mother-in-law, as usual, snagging the slightly better spot! The arms on the chairs are so wide you could balance a cup with ease. Each has a footstool and a perfectly placed cushion for back support. And right beside each chair, there's a little table holding a copy of the *Radio Times*, the TV remote control, and a reading light.

Now, I am not suggesting that we all rush out and buy a huge green leather armchair, or even a La-Z-Boy like Chandler and Joey's from *Friends*. However, I do think that the simple armchair's good points have got a little bit forgotten. So, if you do have a spot for one, do think about the merits of a stylish and comfy armchair. They are, in my opinion, comfortable and underrated!

Whatever you do, don't match your armchair to the sofa! Choose them in an interesting fabric, keep within your colour palette, and add some pattern if you want to. Go vintage, even; there are so many options to choose from.

The underrated armchair.

# An occasional chair

There is a little chair that I could never be without. It goes by various names—occasional chair, accent chair, spare chair, or even an odd-one-out chair! These chairs are the perfect addition to any living room. If you don't have the space, you can pop one in a nearby hallway, ready and waiting to be drawn up for an extra guest when needed. Plus, they are also fantastic for design purposes, as they offer the perfect opportunity to decorate with a fabric that might be a little offbeat.

# Chairs don't like to be alone

Now that we are comfortably seated, let's consider accessorising our seating, building up those layers in the room. While cushions and throws are an essential, chairs also benefit from other accessories. One way to approach chair styling is to view them as social beings; they don't like to be left alone and enjoy the company of tables and lamps! Thus, wherever there's a chair, it should ideally be accompanied by a table and often a lamp too.

This trick is fabulous for design, allowing us to create little vignettes wherever there's a chair!

Table keeps the armchair company!

# The tables

## Coffee tables

In my view, every sofa benefits from having a coffee table positioned just in front of it, if there is space, of course. It can offer another focal point to the room, taking a little attention away from the sofa.

In fact, a living room is in danger of feeling a little incomplete without a coffee table, especially as it has the ability to fill what could otherwise be an awkward empty space. Whether round or rectangular, vintage or modern, traditional wood or sleek glass, trunk or ottoman—they are invariably a wonderful addition.

Styling your coffee table: Whilst there is no one-size-fits-all approach to coffee table styling—here are some ideas for ways to breathe that life and personality into any coffee table, regardless of its shape or size.

I love styling tables!

Add coffee-table books to the table; stack them in varying heights. These are the foundation for the rest of the styling!

Pop items like candles or small bowls on top of the books. This gives them a bit of height and stops them getting lost on the table.

Group items in odd numbers: one candle, three tealights, or a plant with a bowl and a candle.

Add warmth in the shape of candles or little lamps. This just makes the space inviting.

Add a statement piece—a sculpture or decorative bowl will give a focal point.

And to make it all cohesive—keep to your colour palette, but vary the textures and the heights of the things on your table.

## Other tables

Place side tables at each end of your sofa—remembering that they absolutely don't have to match. These tables are the perfect spots for an extra lamp. Style them up by adding a vase of flowers, a simple ornament, or a couple of books, and you've quickly created a lovely little vignette.

And then find room for some occasional tables. Scatter them around your room. Much like their counterpart, occasional chairs, these tables hold a special place in my heart. I have many small, low, simple, usually round tables. They can do anything! If side tables exist for lamps, then these tables exist to accessorise. One day, mine might hold a drink, the next a vase of flowers, another time, some tealights. Since they are so handy and movable, you can never have too many. Place one next to any chair to stop it feeling lonely.

These little tables are wonderful for adding that relaxed informality to a room. And they are perfect pieces for experimenting with that mixy-matchy old and new look, because you can find them anywhere. Department stores have lovely options at reasonable prices, and vintage flea markets are treasure troves, offering everything from little nests of three to tiny round marble ones.

Tables and flowers and lights

# Footstools

I honestly believe that you can't be sitting comfortably if you don't have happy feet! And that's where a footstool comes into play. Pulled up next to the sofa in the evening, it makes the perfect resting spot for those tired toes. But it's also an excellent way to add some interesting pattern or texture to a Relax Max sitting room. If risking a patterned or floral sofa is too much, add it to a footstool; it's a really good place to start. As a bonus, a footstool can double up as a coffee table. Add a huge tray to the top, throw on some books and a candle, and voila!

# Lamps

Layer those lamps. Plop them on those tables and place larger ones on the floor; add them to empty corners and place them at a multitude of heights. Go oversized for a statement piece and add tealights and candles for some flickering feel-good warmth. Keep them within your colour palette, use them as accents, and then have fun with all the textures and styles you can find.

# Rugs

Nothing says softness and sumptuousness in a sitting room quite like a large rug. However, its essential that it be a big one. It should sit in front of the sofa, comfortably accommodating the coffee table, and ideally reaching the other chairs in the room. A huge rug serves as an anchor, a layer of pattern or texture, and a cosiness enhancer too!

# Pull your furniture off the walls

A shelf behind the sofa adds depth

If you want to style your living room so that it looks cool, do *not* push all your furniture against the walls like you are at a teenage disco; try pulling it away a bit. An easy way to start is to place your coffee table in the centre of the room, use that as the focal point, and then arrange the chairs and other furnishings around it to create a comfortable seating area.

In a smaller room, you can still achieve a good layout by simply moving your sofa a foot away from the wall. This tiny adjustment will, believe me, make a big difference to the overall feel of the room.

Add a narrow shelf, or console tables, to those spaces behind the sofa. Fill them with some art, a lamp, and a vase of flowers, and you've automatically added an extra layer of interest and personality to your space. Don't be afraid to shove a chair in front of a bookcase, either; it just adds that extra depth of field.

# Chapter 10

# Kitchens, not just for cooking

*A lot of what you own in a kitchen can be very personal to you.*

When I think of kitchens, I think of my mum. Partly because she and I spent so much of our lives chatting together in that room, but mostly because she was a professional kitchen designer. Unlike her daughter, Mum was incredibly precise, neat, and conscious of fine detail. Her kitchens were perfectly planned to the exact millimetre. Armed with her retractable, "snap-back" tape measure, and a pin-sharp pencil behind her ear, she designed kitchens that made efficient use of space and were functionally brilliant.

Of course, we all need a well-designed kitchen. These are rooms that have a strong functional requirement—storing, preparing, cooking, and eating—just as my mum designed them. But it would be a gross misunderstanding to consider kitchens simply utilitarian places. Spend any time in a kitchen with other people, and you realise how that room has a unique sense of humanity about it. The way people interact in a kitchen is often very different to how they are in the other rooms in a house.

There is a different dynamic.

---

A kitchen with a personality!

Firstly, there is usually some kind of activity happening—often preparing food—over which people are talking or helping each other. So, the conversation can be often more casual and indirect. People are sharing in a task, or just being together as something is being created, even if it is just a bowl of pasta. Unlike every other room, at least one person, if not everyone, will be standing up! So, it's a space where people can relate in a dynamic way, filled with movement and tasks. We connect differently when we are chopping and chatting, sipping and sharing, bustling and babbling.

I've noticed how this casualised atmosphere can often make it easier for my teenagers to share little snippets of their own day or express their worries. Sometimes it's easier to say things to each other when we are just brewing the tea or stirring the pot. And all that is possible before we even sit down and share a meal with each other.

So, what I am trying to encourage is a view of kitchens as so much more than a functional utilitarian space. There is much truth in the old saying that "the kitchen is the heart of the home." So, let's decorate and style it in recognition of it.

Kitchens are a hive of activity.

# Kitchen charisma

Here are some ways in which I feel one can bring out the humanity in a kitchen, creating a Relax Max personality and atmosphere.

## Don't hide everything in a cupboard

Admittedly, there is a lot of stuff in a kitchen, and not always the most visually exciting stuff. So, there is a temptation to have everything out of sight, especially when empty worktops can seem like a signal of a neat and tidy person who has the house under control.

The danger is that you end up with everything squirrelled away behind cupboard doors, leaving you with a rather soulless, minimalist space. So don't deliberately create a kitchen where you put everything away. Remember, a lot of what you own in a kitchen can be very personal to you. The olive bowl you bought last summer on holiday, the teapot from your granny. Make these things visible. By showing them, you are also showing you, and your story.

Use shelves; they are certainly more visually interesting and varied than the sight of cupboard doors. They can be such a beautiful way to showcase small collections of vases, colourful tableware, or tea services. Use open shelving on a wall to help alleviate the dense feel of long cupboards. It makes a kitchen feel a bit lighter and less harsh.

Shelving, not cupboards!

## Fill the floor

Kitchen floors typically feature neutral colours and are usually tiled or made of wood. Whilst these floors are easy to clean and navigate, they have the potential to feel cold, both physically and emotionally, in a room which is predominantly sharp, angular, and hard. So, it is worth including a plan for how you can use your kitchen floor to create a warmer and more characterful room.

You might not imagine using rugs in a kitchen, but I would recommend them highly. Even in the tiniest of kitchens, a small one will warm up a limited floor space. But whatever the size, rugs will provide welcome warmth, colour, and comfort to a cold kitchen floor. On a wintry morning, they feel so much nicer under your feet as you enjoy your first cup of tea of the day. You can buy washable ones nowadays, but mine just are just vacuum-cleaned.

I have a Moroccan rug in front of my dinner table and a runner in front of the cooker.

## Manage the light

Lighting in a kitchen is quite bright, of course, because you need to be able to see what you are doing. But it is often quite harsh too, creating dark corners. So, think about adding some other lighting, just as you might use in the sitting room.

Patterned lampshades are a fabulous way to add texture and colour to a kitchen, and don't forget about those battery-operated lights if you need to pop one on a gloomy shelf. If you are designing from scratch, think about lamps to hang over an island or the kitchen table, and have them on dimmers so that it is easy to change the mood from industrious to social.

## Warm the walls

Traditionally, we don't think of a kitchen's walls as a space for anything in particular. Maybe some functional butcher's hook to hang the outsize saucepans, ladles, and colanders. Maybe some children's drawings from school.

What helps me here is to think a little differently. Instead of thinking about the kitchen as a cooking space that needs something on the walls, I sometimes imagine it as an art gallery where I happen to do some cooking! This mindset opens up more characterful opportunities for styling.

This doesn't mean buying expensive art, or big canvas pieces. Affordable pictures (often from vintage shops) can work really well. You don't need to be fussy about professional placement and lighting, of course. Those sticky picture-hanging strips make it very easy to experiment with different places to put your art.

Books and art can go in a kitchen.

## Books, not just for cooking

Cookery books are not just for culinary inspiration. They can add a sense of personality and texture to the room. So, think about how you display them. Have a few on a countertop with some flowers, or with tea lights on top. Add some more books to a shelf, without simply placing them neatly in a row.

# Kitchen comfort

Kitchen chairs are mostly thought of as the places where you sit to eat, placed at the table or as stools at the bar. But, as I said earlier, a huge proportion of our time in the kitchen isn't spent eating! A kitchen is a lovely place to relax whilst waiting for the soup to boil, or to chat to the "chef." So, see if you can include a more comfortable, relaxed chair in the space, much as you do for your sitting room.

At home, my kitchen is long and thin, with a dining table at one end and the cooker at the other. It obviously isn't big enough to fit a sofa. However, I have found the space for a comfy chair in a little corner, ensuring a spot where people can chat from it, or drink that cup of tea in comfort at any time of day. More importantly, it offers a warm welcome for Twiglet, to curl up on!

# Kitchen kooky

In some ways, the kitchen is a great opportunity to push your styling and decorating boundaries. It's meant to be a room about creation, pleasure, and enjoyment. So have fun with it. Think of it as a place for amusement. Risk a little.

I decided to bring some humour to some of my kitchen lights.

I chose three China-coloured teapot-shaped lamps; each one is a different teapot shape to the others. They are hung asymmetrically from long ropes in the ceiling over the kitchen table. They bring a levity and a smile to your face when you see them.

I also feature two lights in the shape of pigeons: one grey, one yellow. These I placed high up on a shelf, very close to the ceiling. It is my pigeon coop in the kitchen sky! You only really see them when you look up, so it's a very fun, visual reward for those who do.

# Food is colour

Food colouring!

Kitchens are rarely considered colourful places, in contrast to the humanity that goes on within them. The colour scheme is often dominated by the silver and white kitchen appliances. So, it can make a huge difference when even a small number of brighter colours make an appearance.

Fruit and vegetables are your colourful friends! For food that does not need refrigeration, consider it a candidate for its looks, not just its taste; bright red tomatoes, polished green peppers, deep purple onions, a blood-red orange. Place them on your workshops and tables; they don't need to be neat!

# Bring it to the table

Vintage cabbage-leaf
butter dish and knife.

We've spent time in this chapter talking about the kitchen as a whole, but of course it is the dinner table that is the most exciting canvas on which to "paint" your style and character. Styling a table is such a powerful way to provide a gorgeous atmosphere for your guests who dine with you. And it will be a different way every time.

When I have friends around for dinner, I style my table to make the evening feel a little special, but also relaxed and casual. I want to create a table that looks stunningly beautiful, but with a sense of informality. Here are a few tips I regularly use to help achieve that appearance.

# Flowers and food

Flowers help heighten the sense of colour, freshness, and naturalness at a dining table; all welcome qualities when you are sitting down to eat. Consider putting a few small vases with seasonal flowers all the way down the centre of the table. These provide a line of natural beauty and a hint of dining alfresco.

Sweet styling.

Flowers and food.

## Candles forever

It doesn't need to be a birthday to get out the candles! They of course create pools of flickering light at the table to bring some intimacy and atmosphere. Mix up tall candles and tea lights for variation in texture as to how their light is cast across the table.

## Mismatched tableware

A Relax Max table would always avoid the "matching luggage" approach to tableware. Take joy in bringing variety when comes to your pieces.

Add those vintage pieces you have been collecting: bowls, platters, jugs. Old blue-and-white pottery with a willow pattern design, will work on any table. They will all feel different, but in a beautifully coherent way. So picking these up whenever you see them is always a good idea. There are so many pretty glasses to be found now—vintage and new. They are gorgeous and sparkly finishing touches to any table.

## Use fruit to decorate

We have already mentioned using food as a way to create a look and atmosphere in the kitchen—never truer than at the table itself. Blueberries are my particular favourite. Having them overflowing from bowls, spilling onto a tablecloth, provides a little bit of imperfection and casualness.

Flowers and food.

Chapter 11

# Bedrooms, not just for sleeping

*Create your " Sunday morning easy"*

When you are in a bedroom, you are essentially in one of three possible modes: winding down ready for sleep, sleeping, or getting up and ready for the day. Since these modes can be quite different, how should you design your bedroom to make it work equally well for all three?

My advice is not to try! It is hard to style a room that is as good for winding down and sleeping as it is for waking up and getting dressed. Instead, I think of the styling challenge differently. For me, a Relax Max bedroom should be created for a mood, not a mode! It should have an ambience and feel that can work well for whatever time of day or night.

The mood I try to create might be best described as "Sunday morning easy"; relaxed, calm, clear-headed, without being soporific. Giving a bedroom that "Sunday morning easy" vibe will work any day of the week, and feel good at nine o'clock at night or nine in the morning.

Inevitably, the focus of any bedroom will the bed itself, and so I recommend starting your styling there and working out towards the rest of the room.

---

Create a Sunday morning lie-in vibe.

# The bed

The bed is likely to be the largest item in your bedroom, especially if you are a fan of big beds like me! So, it is important to give it the attention it deserves without it completely dominating the space. Let's have a look at how you style a bed from different perspectives.

## On the bed

Decorate the bed, not just the bedroom.

## Duvets

Here is a really simple trick to immediately make your bed look super stylish. The size of your duvet makes a big difference to how a bed can look and feel.

Common sense says you buy a duvet that is the same size as your bed so that it fits! Yet this neat symmetry has the effect of conveying a degree of formality and precision. It lacks character or any sense of indulgence for our "easy Sunday" space. Instead, you want a duvet and cover that is in fact bigger than your bed. You don't want it to fit neatly. It should almost touch the floor on each side of the bed, and should feel like it has enveloped the bed, inviting you to cocoon yourself inside. This brings a sense of generous comfort, a cosy vibe and—reportedly—even leads to better sleep, especially if you are sharing!

So never compromise on the size of your duvet. Many companies now offer oversized duvet covers, but if you can't find one, don't hesitate to size up (which may mean a new duvet, too). For example, use a king-size duvet on a queen bed, or a super-king on a king.

## Linen

I like beds that look like they aren't trying too hard. Linen bedlinen is my go-to. Whilst it isn't cheap, it looks and feels natural and soft. As it doesn't need ironing, it offers a lovely rumpled, carefree vibe that says, "I don't waste much time on household chores!" It's also worth adding that linen is a lovely material to sleep under.

I use a bit of pattern on a bed to break up an otherwise large expanse of material. I love, love, love gingham or stripes— they seem nostalgic, reminiscent of a golden age, but never sentimental! If you want to use a plain duvet, then add a bit of pattern or texture with a colourful throw and a cushion.

## Cushions

Be careful not to use too many cushions on a bed. It creates a formal feel, and you know you only have to remove them every night and replace them every morning. That's not the easy vibe we are aiming for! Just a couple of cushions, simply styled, works for me. They are useful for propping yourself up when reading a book.

# The head of the bed

It is easy to forget about headboards when buying a bed, but they can be a powerful focal point in a bedroom and hugely influence the vibe. There is so much choice—natural wood, painted wood, wicker, upholstered—so spend time looking at the options.

If you can't find a bed with a headboard you like, then a trick I often use is to buy a bed without a headboard and then add one I love. I've found a lovely vintage one on eBay, a wicker one from an online store, and I have created one out of something interesting—those old French shutters. In the small bedroom on page 192, I've built a tongue-and-groove headboard with a little shelf included. It imbues some personality into the wall and provides another styling opportunity, plus it gives a little extra storage space—a bonus!

So, embrace your creativity when deciding on a headboard. It's a real chance to infuse your bedroom with a touch of individuality which adds to that easy Sunday feel.

French shutters as headboard.

# Next to the bed

## Bedside tables

Bedside tables are a golden opportunity to break free from convention and express your creativity again!

Whatever you do, don't match them to your bed, and you don't need to match them to each other either! Your bedroom is not a formal hotel room, and we are not trying to create a coordinated bedroom suite!

If you are going for the mix-and-match look, think of that asymmetric styling again and choose those tables that are different from each other but have a unifying element that ties them together. You are looking for a touch of unity, with a big dose of individuality.

Bedside tables also don't have to be new. They are without doubt one of those pieces of furniture where a little bit of history and worn patina adds to their character and brings a little charm to a bedroom.

They need not be sold as bedside tables at all. You can reimagine bedside tables from so many things. Think vintage desk or old school chair, an old trunk or an occasional table in cool material. Decorate them with a little vase, a lamp, and very little else.

## Bedside lights

Bedside lights offer a similar opportunity for creativity. If you are a fan of lamps, the bedroom is the perfect spot to experiment and mix up the styles.

If you are opting for mismatched bedside tables, you might consider maintaining some uniformity with a matching pair of lamps to introduce some harmony. But if you decide to mix it up entirely, the usual rules apply—find an element of similarity to tie them together!

If you are short on space, don't hesitate to hang your bedside lights from the ceiling. I love this look, and it's a stylish solution that helps to declutter a bedside table. Importantly, I feel that specifically hanging lights should not be mismatched. Even I have limits of asymmetry in a house!

## Rugs

If you have the space, always put a rug next to the bed. It creates that feeling of warmth and comfort, and it is always lovely to snuggle your toes into on a cold morning.

---

Little bedside lamps.

## At the end of the bed

Another simple trick to elevate your bedroom to the next level is to pop something like a bench, a little sofa, or a blanket box at the end of the bed. It's a styling trick that, like a headboard, draws the attention from the bed and encourages your eye to move across the room. It's a great excuse to add a little bit of vintage, as well as giving you that extra bit of essential bedroom storage.

# Beyond the bed

## Chairs

Every bedroom should contain a bed, but also a chair! The inclusion of a chair has the effect of making the room feel bigger than just the dominating bed. It also provides extra pattern, texture, and variation across the space. Look for small accent chairs (or even a little sofa if you have the space). I love my little wicker chair positioned by the window, piled with a couple of cushions.

These chairs can also offer a convenient place to hurriedly dump clothes before bed, or be the spot for admiring the view from your window.

## Curtains

Dare I say this? I am not a fan of curtains—well, not the big bulky ones, anyway. If you've been following me on social media, that might not come as a surprise!

Instead, I prefer the practicality and simplicity of blackout blinds that effortlessly roll up and disappear, allowing as much light as possible to flood the room whilst still giving privacy and the option to create proper darkness when needed. Or I opt for whimsical, linen-mix curtains, those that dance in the slightest breeze, keeping the room feeling light and airy for that easy Sunday vibe. Where I do have a whimsical linen curtain, I have a blackout blind behind to provide that functionality when needed.

Blanket box and wicker chair.

Shutters in the mirror.

## Dressing tables and mirrors

Dressing tables, like bedside tables, don't actually have to be bought as dressing tables. Look for a table or desk you love—vintage or modern—and use that as a dressing table. Add a mirror popped on top, style it with trays and vintage plates for your jewellery, and you will have created a stunning, characterful piece.

# Colour

The easy Sunday morning vibe—croissants and sunlight streaming in—
needs a particular kind of colour. For me, the primary colour in my bedroom
should be on the lighter side; a morning colour that gently encourages you
to wake. I would avoid the darker, cocooning colours that might seem to
work best at night-time; they will struggle to work well in the mornings.

A vintage bedroom corner; nothing here is new!

# Getting organised

If there's one room in the house that is prone to clutter, it's the bedroom.

The potential for loose odds and ends, bits and bobs, is endless; makeup, clothes you wear, clothes you have worn, and clothes you have had for years and haven't yet sorted out! Shoes, hair accessories, piles of books, and things that fall out of your pocket at night! All of which means it is easy for a bedroom to look overly messy. Much as we love a bit of personality in a room, we don't want clutter-filled chaos. So, maximise all hidden cupboard and drawer space you can, and then style your clutter as creatively as possible.

Have a hatstand in a corner, or some vintage pegs on an empty wall. Make it a display for scarfs and bags. Hang those straw bags you take to the beach on the pegs; they will look stunning displayed like this, and they provide extra storage too.

Have trays on your dressing table for all the bits. Trays are marvellous styling tools, bringing structure to all those odds and ends. The multitude of skincare bottles will look so much better grouped together on a tray than scattered across the surface of a table. Little vintage bowls are wonderful for holding costume jewellery and hair accessories, whilst necklaces look lovely displayed on a vintage mirror.

# Don't forget

Don't forget to add a little bit of all the other Relax Max things we have talked about previously.

Hang some art above the bed, or really low over the bedside table. Prop a picture casually on the floor. Add some plants. Have a shelf above the bed which is dedicated to some trailing plants, or nestle a big monstera next to your chair. Green plants in a bedroom are good for the soul!

Little painting, hung low.

# Chapter 12

# Bathrooms, not just for bathing

*Think of your bathroom as an extension of the rest of your home*

Bathrooms, like kitchens, are oft-overlooked corners of our homes when it comes to styling. So often they are treated as purely functional spaces, where major fixtures take precedence over the smaller details. We tend to buy everything from a one-stop bathroom shop, where we prioritise our budget on the baths, showers, sinks, and loos. There's no reason why the bathroom cannot be treated in just the same way, with the same attention to those personal touches, as any other room in the house.

The Relax Max approach is, as always, to look for the more emotional dimensions of a room. It turns out that, despite the apparent utilitarian nature of bathrooms, they are in fact quiet emotional places. Many pieces of research have uncovered that one of the biggest benefits of this room is that it is the spot we head to when we need a little bit of time to ourselves, a bit of relief from the goings-on in the rest of the house! The innate privacy of a bathroom means it is a place that can provide some respite from the outside world, to switch off and take stock.

Bathroom as a room.

So, my advice for how to think about styling bathrooms is to think you are creating "five minutes of peace." In reality, people will spend longer or even shorter periods there, but a place that can deliver five minutes of peace will have the right vibe, warmth, and ambience for everyone. Here are some of the ways I love to give my bathroom that feeling.

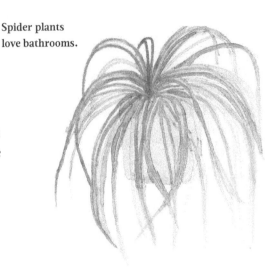

Spider plants love bathrooms.

## Don't shop the bathroom shop

Do consider your bathroom an extension of the rest of your home, and don't be afraid to treat it that way. Whilst bathrooms obviously require many functional items which need to be carefully planned and bought from a speciality shop, it's so important to realise that not everything has to be!

For example, you don't need to buy a mirror for the bathroom in a bathroom shop. In fact, you don't need a "bathroom mirror" at all. You just need a mirror, one that you love, that happens to go in your bathroom. The same is true for storage and even lighting. These items can be found elsewhere and in a style that suits you. Finding ways to incorporate these pieces will immediately stop your bathroom from feeling like a bathroom showroom!

An excellent starting point for finding these pieces for the bathroom is to search for vintage pieces. A few "old" pieces will automatically bring their beautiful warmth and worn patina to the room, softening those clean lines, hard textures, and functional aspects.

An easy start is to swap that standard bathroom mirror for a vintage one. There are so many to choose from, like the French bamboo in my shower room. Vintage mirrors aren't the only option, of course; any mirror that adds a bit of personality to the space will do!

Bathroom storage is without doubt a marvellous way to add some history when all around you is bright and modern. For example, an old medicine cabinet hung on the wall can become the perfect spot to store all those lotions and potions. Alternatively, an antique chest of drawers, or even an old armoire (if you have the space!), will bring warmth as well as provide a place to keep towels. Add a plant and a candle to some rattan shelves for an extra bit of decoration.

It might also be possible to not use a bathroom store to buy some of the bathroom essentials. The basin or sink, for example, is an opportunity to go vintage! You can stand a new basin on top of an old table or desk. Alternatively, consider opting for a colourful vintage sink like the one I have in my own shower room.

Whenever you can, seek out items you love that are not "made for bathrooms," and not bought from bathroom stores, and then put them in your bathroom anyway!

Bathroom storage doesn't have to come from a bathroom shop.

# Shun the shiny

A tiny bathroom full of patterns and textures.

It's all too easy to end up with a bathroom that is dominated by lots of hard, white, shiny surfaces, even shinier than kitchens! The result is often rather plain, cold, and austere. It's hard to find "five minutes of peace" in a space that feels so unforgiving. So the styling challenge is to find a way to counterbalance this clinical feel with personality and style, and blend something new.

The Relax Max approach finds the solution in adding pattern, texture, and colour to soften the shiny, white, and sleek. Let's look at the ways this can be brought into the bathroom space.

## Tiles

Tiles are an obvious way to add some texture and pattern to your bathroom. You can tile your floor in a classic checkerboard design or with tiles that create a beautiful pattern. You can add texture to your walls with some Moroccan zellige tiles or some coloured subway tiles. Whichever you choose, tiles have a huge effect on the feeling of your bathroom—the right ones will automatically infuse it with warmth and character and texture, so they deserve to be given a lot of thought.

Don't overlook simple, budget-friendly tiles, particularly for the shower. You can find them in virtually any colour

and shade nowadays. Opt for a grout that complements the tiles, whether it's a darker shade or a hue that matches the tile itself. Consider placing the tiles as close together as your tiler allows. A skinny grout looks chic! And if you are renting, or on a tight budget, don't dismiss the option of stick-on-tiles. They are definitely worth exploring for a fast, cheap, and removable fix.

## Panelling

I will always have a soft spot for a panelled bathroom. They just exude a timeless elegance that I love, and panelling is a good way to add texture and variation to the walls.

There are many options for panelling, but tongue-and-groove is my all-time favourite. Consider mixing up the widths of the boards to add an extra bit of interest, or even laying it horizontally instead of vertically. If you are adding some panelling, make sure to include a little shelf on top. Not only will it make the perfect spot for a picture, a plant, or a toothbrush, but you can always add some wallpaper above it too!

## Colours

Opting for those soft but warm colours is the ultimate way to create a calm space in a bathroom. Think pale blues, or earthy, stony naturals, or go back to those soft pinks or greens. Whatever your choice, stick firmly to that basic premise of a limited colour palette, ensuring that everything possible ties into it.

I personally love using just two shades of single colour in a bathroom, and incorporating them wherever possible (with an accent colour thrown into the mix for a burst of contrast). These two-tone colour schemes can have a reputation for sometimes being a little unexciting, but I love them for creating that zen-like atmosphere in a bathroom.

## Rugs and mats

Counteract the hard features of a bathroom by adding softness to the room.

If you don't have much space, there are some wonderful fluffy floor mats out there now in all manner of patterns. Remember, they don't have to be specialist bathmats; they can be just lovely mats that you put in the bathroom! It's worth a look. Otherwise, a rug will always add grand style to a bigger bathroom. If you are worried about the damp, consider a washable one. There are a whole host of online retailers who offer those.

## A spot to perch

Surprisingly, in a bathroom, it is sometimes nice to have a place to sit which isn't the loo! So, if you have the space, add a little stool or chair. Not only is it handy, it adds another layer of non-bathroom-y interest.

A vintage pink sink adds interest.

# Lighting

Let's talk about the topic of lighting our bathrooms, because it's another excellent means to infuse that warmth into our space.

Bathrooms require different kinds of lighting. Brighter lighting is needed for certain tasks, like applying makeup. Yet, softer lighting is needed to add that relaxed, soothing atmosphere, so you need to build in some flexibility and employ some varied lighting tactics.

Whilst downlights aren't typically my go-to choice for lighting, they do make sense in bathrooms, as they are often equipped with dimmers to easily change the brightness and mood. However, don't limit yourself to just these; incorporate some different light sources too. Add a wireless lamp with a patterned or textured shade to bring a little bit of style and softness. Or hunt for some of the most delightful bathroom-friendly lights that are out there now. With a little effort, you can find whole ranges of wall and pendant lights that are not sold as bathroom lights but can work equally well in that room.

## The usual suspects

As always, add some more of your personality to your bathroom with the usual suspects.

A piece of art or a vase of flowers perched on a bathroom shelf looks just as lovely here as it does in the bedroom.

Plants are a must; consider hanging a floating shelf above the shower and filling it with greenery.

Books strategically placed besides the loo will always encourage us to linger a little longer.

Add in a tiny vintage vase to hold a toothbrush, or even just a pretty saucer to hold your soap.

It's these personal touches that will make your bathroom into a room that beckons you for five minutes' peace.

Gentle bathroom pinks.

# Chapter 13

# A final note

*Your home represents the real you,*

*with great richness and joy.*

# It's personal

Creating a home is a voyage of discovery, not just in the sense of learning about different styles, fabrics, and colours, but in the constant exploration and expression of oneself through the look and feel of one's home.

Writing this book has helped me really appreciate how styling a home is a form of self-expression. I just couldn't put pen to paper about decorating my home without sharing the stories of the things in it, what they mean to me, and how they came into my life. It is all bound up together; I am my home; my home is me.

From the colours I am drawn to, to the pieces of furniture I have picked up through life's journey, to the memories I've made and the rituals I've created, putting these elements into my home make it truly mine.

As we evolve through life, so that too will be reflected in our homes. The flat I lived in in Notting Hill at twenty was for the 'me' I was then. My house now is for today's 'me.' Who knows how my life and style will shift and evolve, but I suspect I'll always be a Relaxed Maximalist at heart.

In these pages, I have often mentioned the phrase, "a home to make you smile." This of course wasn't about humour, but about a light-heartedness and a feel-good factor. It just feels good when your home truly reflects who you are.

Despite wishing otherwise, I'm not a neat and tidy person, so living in a neat and tidy house would not be a good fit! Orderly minimalism might look good to some people's eyes, but it would not feel good for me!

Our homes should fit us like a much-loved sweater or a warm glove—an effortless, comfortable fit.

Of course, many things allow us to express ourselves, like clothes, makeup, hair, and cars. But for me, a home is the most personal. My home represents the real me, with great richness and joy, more than just a dress or a makeover ever could.

If my personal stories in this book have resonated with you and you've learned a bit along the way, I'm delighted. I hope you find your way to tell your story in your Relax Max home.

Feel free to stay in touch with me and share your journey. I will forever be @ ahometomakeyousmile.

*Sarah x*

# Some thank-yous

I owe the biggest thank-you to my husband Guy, not just for his eternal belief in me, but also for his invaluable roles as my sounding board, first editor, and becoming the most amazing cook. So good, that I might just pretend to be writing this book forever!

To my gorgeous and suddenly grown-up children, Billy and Polly, thank you for your unwavering encouragement, and not-so-subtle nudges whenever I veered off track.

For my mum and dad, who would undoubtedly be bursting with pride if they were here today. The sense of home and love of books that they instilled in me has so deeply influenced how I wanted my own home to be.

Thank you also to my photographer Lou Souza (@lsouza_photography), whose eye for capturing the perfect interiors, portrait, or lifestyle photo made working together an absolute joy.

Thank you to Carlotta Spencer for her gorgeous illustrations, painted over late nights and holidays, all whilst juggling her studies for her architecture degree. You can find her @carchitecturee.

To my brother and sister-in-law Tom and Amber, and their children, Flora and Ralph. Thank you for being the most enthusiastic celebrators of every step on my journey to this point.

To the entire Friend family, thanks for being there over the last ten years, but especially Katie—although this book would have been completed in half the time if it weren't for those hours spent on the telephone!

A very special thanks to my friend Anna @hellosocialmedia, without whom @ahometomakeyousmile wouldn't ever have existed.

For Lucia, I couldn't have done any of this without you by my side.

To all my fabulous friends whom I have seen much less of this past year, but who have been there for me nonetheless.

To Mango Publishing and my editor Natasha. Thanks for the opportunities and for the support, for your patience and the movable deadlines!

And finally, to every single one of my followers. I wouldn't be here without you, and you make my job one I love. Thank you!

# About the Author

Sarah Laming is an interior stylist, interior decorator and content creator with a passion for homes and interiors that has evolved from a hobby to the central focus in her life.

Her working life began in advertising, and then teaching. But about ten years ago, she studied a course on interior decoration at the famous Chelsea College of Arts in London and has been styling interiors ever since.

Sarah began her Instagram account @ahometomakeyousmile just four years ago, and it has grown to over 1.2 million followers in this short space of time. She was one of Pinterest UK's top creators in 2023 and has a big TikTok following too. Her reels and TikToks consistently go viral and have been viewed well over 250 million times around the world. In fact, Pooky Lights recently described her as an "Instagram Interiors Phenomenon."

Sarah regularly works with brands such as Anthropologie, Le Creuset, Piglet in Bed and Samsung on content creation and advises on interior decoration and styling. Her work has been featured in magazines and on blogs. She was named one of the top ten maximalist interiors accounts by *The Spruce* and was one of *Homes and Antiques's* top ten interiors accounts to follow in 2022. *Bustle* magazine described her TikTok account as "Maximalism but with a relaxed twist."

Sarah's style is a laid-back, Relaxed Maximalism. She believes that you should always create a home that makes you smile—one that reflects your personal history and makes you happy. A home that is curated slowly and layered gradually so that it becomes a reflection of you. She doesn't believe that a home can ever be perfect; her own is gloriously perfectly imperfect!

Sarah lives in London with her family and Twiglet, the Cavalier King Charles Spaniel.

Instagram@ahometomakeyousmile
TikTok@ahometomakeyousmile
Pinterest@ahometomakeyousmile

Mango Publishing, established in 2014, publishes an eclectic list of books by diverse authors—both new and established voices—on topics ranging from business, personal growth, women's empowerment, LGBTQ studies, health, and spirituality to history, popular culture, time management, decluttering, lifestyle, mental wellness, aging, and sustainable living. We were named 2019 *and* 2020's #1 fastest growing independent publisher by *Publishers Weekly.* Our success is driven by our main goal, which is to publish high-quality books that will entertain readers as well as make a positive difference in their lives.

Our readers are our most important resource; we value your input, suggestions, and ideas. We'd love to hear from you—after all, we are publishing books for you!

Please stay in touch with us and follow us at:

Facebook: Mango Publishing
Twitter: @MangoPublishing
Instagram: @MangoPublishing
LinkedIn: Mango Publishing
Pinterest: Mango Publishing
Newsletter: mangopublishinggroup.com/newsletter

Join us on Mango's journey to reinvent publishing, one book at a time.